Colloquial Italian

The Colloquial 2 Series

Series Adviser: Gary King

The following languages are available in the Colloquial 2 series:

French
Italian
Russian
Spanish

Accompanying cassettes and CDs are available for the above titles. They can be ordered through your bookseller, or send payment with order to Taylor & Francis/ Routledge Ltd, ITPS, Cheriton House, North Way, Andover, Hants SP10 5BE, UK, or to Routledge Inc, 29 West 35th Street, New York NY 10001, USA.

Colloquial Italian

The next step in language learning

Sylvia Lymbery and Sandra Silipo

Routledge
Taylor & Francis Group

LONDON AND NEW YORK

First published 2003
by Routledge
11 New Fetter Lane, London EC4P 4EE

Simultaneously published in the USA and Canada
by Routledge
29 West 35th Street, New York, NY 10001

Routledge is an imprint of the Taylor & Francis Group

Typeset in Sabon and Helvetica by
Florence Production Ltd, Stoodleigh, Devon

Printed and bound in Great Britain by
Biddles Ltd, Guildford and King's Lynn

British Library Cataloguing in Publication Data
A catalogue record for this book is available from the British Library

Library of Congress Cataloging in Publication Data
Lymbery, Sylvia.
   Colloquial Italian 2: the next step in language learning/Sylvia Lymbery
   and Sandra Silipo.
   p. cm. – (The colloquial 2 series)
Includes index.
1. Italian language – Conversation and phrase books – English.
2. Italian language – Textbooks for foreign speakers – English.   3. Italian
language – Spoken Italian.   I. Title: Colloquial Italian two.   II. Silipo,
Sandra, 1967– .   III. Title. IV. Series.
   PC1121 .L96 2003
   458.3'421–dc21   2002154532

ISBN 0–415–28154–7 (book)
ISBN 0–415–28155–5 (audio cassette)
ISBN 0–415–28157–1 (audio CD)
ISBN 0–415–28156–3 (pack)

Contents

Acknowledgements   vii
How to use this book   ix

Unit 1   **Presentiamoci!**   1
          Let's introduce ourselves!

Unit 2   **Di dove sei?**   14
          Where do you come from?

Unit 3   **Che tipo sei?**   26
          What sort of person are you?

Unit 4   **Che cosa pensi di me?**   39
          What's your opinion of me?

Unit 5   **Ci siamo incontrati così**   52
          This is how we met

Unit 6   **Studi e carriera**   65
          Education and career

Unit 7   **Lavorare in Italia**   77
          Working in Italy

Unit 8   **Un colloquio di lavoro**   90
          An interview for a job

Unit 9   **La famiglia sta cambiando**   106
          The family is changing

Unit 10   **Nord e Sud**   119
          North and South

Unit 11   **L'italiano e i suoi dialetti**   130
          Italian and its dialects

Unit 12   **Essere italiani**   146
          Being Italian

Appendix 1 Background   162
Appendix 2 Dialects and minority languages   168
Grammar reference   174
Key to exercises   192
Grammar index   210

Acknowledgements

We should like to express our thanks to those who have helped us, notably: the people who kindly gave their time to be interviewed; Raffaella Silipo and Angioletta Viviani who wrote pieces for the book at our request; Sandra's students in Norwich who tried out much of the material and in particular Gill Hood, who kindly read everything for us – all made useful suggestions; the Editor of *La Stampa* for permission to use a number of articles and photos; the Editor of *Il Corriere della Sera*, for permission to use an article, photo and table; to the publishers of *Lo Zingarelli* for permission to quote a number of definitions from the dictionary. We have tried to trace the publishers of the Sicilian poet Ignazio Butitta (1899–1997) for permission to reproduce part of his dialect poem but at the time of writing have not managed to do so.

In addition, we both owe much to family and friends. Sandra would like to thank Richard, her parents and her sister for all their support and practical help and Sylvia is similarly grateful to Charlotte and to friends.

Italy, showing the regions and the regional capitals

How to use this book

Colloquial Italian 2 seeks to follow the spirit of *Colloquial Italian*: to guide the independent learner to a surer grasp of Italian. You need some knowledge of Italian to use this book but not necessarily gained from using *Colloquial Italian*. You may have used another book for beginners, attended an evening class, or perhaps visited Italy often, lived there maybe. Whatever your experience, you have some knowledge and want to build on it. This book helps you to do that. The book may well be of interest to more advanced learners: it is often helpful to meet points presented in a different way or simply to read new material.

Colloquial Italian 2 contains materials on a variety of topics; all the materials are authentic, either captured in conversations with Italian speakers or taken from articles from Italian newspapers. In two cases Italians have written material for the book on specific subjects at our request. We have edited where we thought necessary, but you will find the material ranges from the straightforward to the challenging. Each unit focuses on a particular topic and several give you glimpses of life in Italy at the start of the twenty-first century. Much of the material is also recorded, so that you can work on spoken Italian too. In addition to that, there is a web site to support the Colloquial courses. At http://www.routledge.com/colloquials/italian you will find extra exercises as well as links to sites that build on the material in the units.

The dialogues and texts are followed by notes to help you with potentially difficult points. Each unit explains a number of Language points, often going over points you may have met, always a valuable activity, since each time you find you understand and remember better. Some Language points will be new to you. The Language points are usually backed up by exercises to help you learn the new material. And we also make Language learning suggestions based on our experience as language learners ourselves, as well as language teachers. Not all will suit you – language learners differ just as people generally do. We hope you will find some which are helpful to you.

The units probably contain too much material to be covered in one session, so don't be afraid to break them up – perhaps the text one day, a Language point and an exercise the next. Much depends on the time you have available – and on you, what sort of learner you are. Just do it your way!

Language learning is challenging and at times we all feel we are not making progress. Try not to get downhearted. Try to keep finding the time, moving forward a little. You *will* get better. And that will open windows for you on to new experiences. We hope you will be able to enjoy at first hand the fruits of your efforts by a visit to Italy. Travelling to a country whose language you know, however imperfectly, is a pleasure that is not to be missed. Italy is a country that has been a magnet for travellers since the days of the Grand Tour and has much to offer. Beyond the obvious, such as the beautiful and varied scenery, the art treasures, the food and wine, and the cordiality and generosity which you will find when you make Italian friends, there is a complex and fascinating nation. And even if you can't visit Italy yet, it is something to look forward to and you have unlocked the door to a new and rich culture, to new and interesting people to meet. Enjoy your studies!

1 Presentiamoci!

In this unit you will

▶ meet some Italians
▶ check your knowledge of the form and use of the present tense: regular verbs
▶ look at the use of **da** and the present tense
▶ revise numbers and dates
▶ practise talking about yourself

Dialogues

Sandra interviews two fellow Italians living in England.

Exercise 1

The interviews which follow are recorded on the cassette and we suggest you:

• read the questions below
• listen to the recording once or twice without looking at the written text
• try to answer the questions
• listen again, this time looking at the text

You can check your answers in the Key to exercises at the back of the book.

1 Whose family name doesn't sound Italian at all? Is it?
2 Which speaker knows three foreign languages?
3 Which speaker has been living in England for less than a year?

Dialogue 1

TERESA   Mi chiamo Teresa, sono italiana, sono di Napoli, sono nata
              a Napoli, e adesso vivo qui a Norwich da più di cinque anni,
              in Inghilterra. Studio all'università dell'East Anglia e faccio
              un dottorato.
SANDRA   In che cosa?
TERESA   In traduzione letteraria.
SANDRA   Quindi conosci le lingue?
TERESA   Conosco l'inglese, il francese e il greco moderno.

Francesca

Dialogue 2

FRANCESCA   Mi chiamo Francesca, Francesca Tonzig, sono di
              Padova, ho 28 anni, e vivo qui a Norwich per studio, per
              motivi di studio.
SANDRA   Da quando?
FRANCESCA   Da Pasqua. Quindi sono . . . quanti? . . . sei mesi.
SANDRA   Il tuo cognome non suona italiano.
FRANCESCA   Allora il mio cognome . . . come primo impatto non
              sembra italiano. E' perché viene da una città che si
              chiama Gorizia, che è vicina al confine con la Slovenia.
              Quindi ha qualche radice slava, croata. In realtà ci sono
              molti cognomi di questo genere nell'area di Trieste,
              Trieste e Gorizia. Finiscono in 'ich'. Adesso non mi
              viene in mente nessun esempio . . . Ah sì però, tipo

Sgombrovich. Sgombrovich è un giocatore di pallacanestro, che è italianissimo, però ha questo cognome che sembra quasi russo . . . in quell'area geografica, che è di frontiera, ci sono molte famiglie che sono completamente italiane, però il nome . . . sembra più slavo. In realtà sono famiglie italianissime.

Vocabulary ♦

ho 28 anni	I am 28 (years old)
avere x anni	to be x years old
non mi viene in mente	I can't think of one (lit. one doesn't come into my mind; 'one' being an example of a name)
tipo Sgombrovich	like Sgombrovich (**tipo** used instead of **come** is common in spoken Italian)
nome / cognome	first, given name/surname

Language points ♦

Revision of the present tense: form

Exercise 2

Check your knowledge of the present tense by completing the following sentences about the people you met above. Use the verbs listed in the box. They are not in the right order and can be used more than once.

> Example: **Teresa** _____ **italiana.**
> **Teresa è italiana.**

> vivere conoscere venire finire essere fare avere
> sembrare chiamarsi studiare suonare

1 La prima persona _____ Teresa. _____ di Napoli ma adesso _____ a Norwich. _____ all'università, _____ un dottorato in traduzione letteraria, quindi _____ le lingue. _____ a Norwich da più di cinque anni.

2 Francesca _____ un cognome che non suona italiano. Questo perché il suo cognome _____ da Gorizia. Nell'area di Trieste ci _____ molti cognomi che _____ quasi russi perché _____ in 'ich'. Il cognome di Francesca _____ in 'ig', che è simile.

- Check your answers in the Key to exercises at the back of the book. The present of regular verbs should be familiar to you. There are three main types, classified according to the ending of the infinitive: -are, -ere, -ire. The -ire group subdivides in the present tense. In the Grammar reference, in addition to a table showing the three types of verb, there is a list of common -ire verbs of each subgroup.

- Verbs are traditionally set out in tables vertically in columns. We usually learn a verb 'going down', e.g.: **parlo, parli, parla, parliamo, parlate, parlano**. Some people find it more useful to consider them 'going across', e.g.: **parlo, scrivo, dormo, finisco**. This highlights the similarities and differences between the various types of regular verb.

- Working across, you can see that there is no difference between the endings of some persons of the verb from one type to another:

    1st person singular: always ends in -o
    2nd person singular: always ends in -i
    1st person plural: always ends in -iamo

You may find it helpful to highlight the differences between the verb types and concentrate on them.

- An important point: the verb ending carries information about the subject of the verb; in other words, it does what the words *I, you, we*, etc. do in English.

I live – **vivo**   We live – **viviamo**

Exercise 3

Complete the table below. All the verbs are regular in the present tense. Where the stress in the verb falls irregularly, mark it.

Check your answers in the verb table in the Grammar reference. All the verbs in the exercise are there, some in the notes. If you feel you need to, take time to revise the form of the present tense now.

	parlare	mangiare	scrivere	leggere	dormire	finire
io *(1st person singular)*	parlo	———	———	———	———	———
tu *(2nd person singular)*	———	mangi	———	———	———	———
lui / lei *(3rd person singular)*	———	———	scrive	———	———	———
noi *(1st person plural)*	———	———	———	leggiamo	———	———
voi *(2nd person plural)*	———	———	———	———	dormite	———
loro *(3rd person plural)*	———	———	———	———	———	fin/scono

Revision of the present tense: uses

1. As well as translating the one-word English present, the present in Italian can be used when in English we would use a present continuous:

Vivo a Norwich.
I live in Norwich.

Sono di Napoli ma ora vivo a Norwich.
I am from Naples but now I am living in Norwich.

Faccio un dottorato.
I am studying for a PhD.

Italian also has a present continuous: **Sto facendo un dottorato** is possible. We will return to this in Unit 6 and Unit 9.

2. In spoken Italian, the present is often used with future meaning, expressing intention and often when in English we might say: 'going to' + verb.

Che cosa fai domani?
What are you doing / going to do tomorrow?

Domani lavoro tutto il giorno.
Tomorrow I am going to work / I'm working all day.

Ti telefono quando arrivo.
I will ring you when I get there.

(For the future and more on this point, see also Unit 9.)

3. The present tense with **da** and an expression of time: to say someone 'has been doing' something for a certain amount of time or since a certain point in time – and with the implication that he/she is still doing it – in Italian you use the **present** tense of the verb and **da**. If you are asking a question, it is normally: **da quanto tempo, da quanto?** ('for how long?') or **da quando?** (lit. 'since when?')

Note: In spoken Italian, **da quando** is often used instead of **da quanto** meaning 'for how long'. You don't have to worry if you happen to choose the wrong one.

Francesca, da quanto vivi a Norwich?
Francesca how long have you been living / have you lived in Norwich?

Vivo a Norwich da tre mesi.
I have been living in Norwich for three months.

Francesca, da quando vivi a Norwich?
Francesca since when have you been living / have you lived in Norwich?

Vivo a Norwich da Pasqua.
I have been living in Norwich since Easter.

Da quanto studi l'italiano?
Since when have you been studying / learning Italian?

Studio l'italiano da due anni.
I have been studying / learning Italian for two years.

Da quando studi l'italiano?
How long have you been studying / learning Italian?

Studio l'italiano dall'anno* scorso.
I have been studying Italian since last year.

*Note: The 'l' is doubled before the vowel, as is usual when **da** is combined with **l'**.

Exercise 4

Ask the following questions in Italian and use the information in brackets to answer.

> Example: Teresa, how long have you been living in England? (4 years)
> **Teresa, da quanto tempo vivi in Inghilterra? Vivo in Inghilterra da quattro anni.**

1 Teresa, how long have you been living in Norwich? (5 or 6 years)
2 Teresa, how long have you been doing your PhD? (3 years)
3 Francesca, since when have you been studying French? (Natale)
4 Francesca, how long have you been working as an interpreter? (6 months)

Text

You will probably have seen Lavazza coffee for sale, even if you have not bought it. Here is something of the story behind the company which is one of the best known coffee suppliers in Italy. And coffee, you will be aware, has a very special place in Italian life.

Exercise 5

Read the questions and then read the text, looking for the answers. It is not necessary to understand every word to get the main points of the article.

1 What made Luigi Lavazza leave Murisengo and go to Turin?
2 Why did Luigi Lavazza feel the need to move to bigger premises in 1910?
3 How many actual coffee shops does the Lavazza firm own?
4 A new packaging material was introduced in 1915. What advantage did it have?
5 What other significant event in the company's history occurred in 1915?

6 Why was the company in a state of crisis between 1939 and 1945?
7 What significant step did Emilio Lavazza take in 1980?
8 What honour did the company receive in 1998? How old was the company by then?

I signori del caffè

La famiglia Lavazza ha contribuito a diffondere nel mondo la tradizione del caffè italiano grazie ad un'impresa che oggi è tra le prime al mondo.

Luigi Lavazza, nato a Murisengo, un paese del Monferrato alessandrino, il 24 aprile del 1859, è uno dei 'Signori del caffè' della importante tradizione del gusto e dell'aroma del nostro Paese.

Nel 1885, spronato dal padre, agricoltore, a cercare una vita meno dura, Luigi Lavazza lascia il paese natio con sole 50 lire in tasca (l'equivalente di circa 150 euro odierni) e si trasferisce a Torino.

Nel 1894 rileva una drogheria dissestata nel centro storico di Torino e, appena un anno più tardi, nel 1895, sancisce la nascita ufficiale della Lavazza, che diventerà uno dei fiori all'occhiello dell'Italia. Nel 1910 l'attività si è ormai ampliata ed è necessario trasferirla in locali più ampi, e precisamente al numero 10 di via San Tommaso, dove si trova oggi l'unico Caffè al mondo di proprietà di Lavazza.

Nel 1915 l'azienda è al primo posto tra le imprese italiane importatrici e torrefattrici di caffè. Inizia la costruzione di una nuova sede in corso Giulio Cesare e adotta un nuovo materiale di confezionamento che consente la conservazione dell'aroma e della fragranza del caffè tostato.

Nel 1933, all'età di 74 anni, Luigi Lavazza cede tutte le sue azioni della società ai figli Mario, Beppe e Pericle che assumono la conduzione dell'azienda. Nel 1939 Mussolini ordina il blocco delle importazioni di caffè, che continuerà fino al 1945 determinando una crisi profonda nell'azienda.

Nel 1971 Emilio Lavazza succede come amministratore delegato alla morte del padre Beppe e nel 1980 istituisce il Centro Luigi Lavazza per gli Studi e le Ricerche sul Caffè, impegnato sul terreno culturale e nella ricerca scientifica. Da qui nasce il 'Training Centre', la scuola del caffè di Lavazza.

Successivamente la Lavazza decide di sbarcare in diversi paesi in tutto il mondo: nel 1987 fonda a Francoforte Lavazza Deutschland GmbH, nel 1988 la Lavazza Premium Coffee a New York e Lavazza Kaffee SA a Vienna.

Nel 1991 entra in azienda Giuseppe, figlio di Emilio, attualmente nel Consiglio di Amministrazione. Quattro anni dopo arriva finalmente il 1995, l'anno del Centenario e arriva anche, nel 1998, l'ultimo atto nella storia dell'azienda: Lavazza diventa il caffè ufficiale della Coppa del Mondo di Calcio (Francia '98).

Source: Vincenzo Palatella, *News Italia Press*
Adapted from: *I Grandi Italiani nel Mondo: I Signori del Caffè*, www.e-italici.org

Vocabulary ♦

Note: In the Vocabulary lists, italics indicate which words or sentences have not been used in the texts, but may be helpful.

paese / Paese	village or nation, state (With this latter meaning it is often written with a capital letter: **Il Bel Paese** often = Italy. In the former meaning, often: **paese natio** = village *or* town of birth)
il Monferrato	an attractive hilly area to the east and south-east of Turin
alessandrino	in the area of Alessandria, a large town to the east of Turin
spronato	spurred on
uno sperone	a spur (*verb*: **spronare**)
150 euro odierni	150 euros in today's money
odierno	of today (the article appears to have been written around 2000)
rileva una drogheria dissestata	he bought a run-down grocer's shop
sancisce (sancire)	to ratify, make legal (works like **capire**)

uno dei fiori all'occhiello	un fiore all'occhiello is something to be proud of (lit. a flower in a buttonhole. In English perhaps: a feather in one's cap)
imprese ... torrefattrici	coffee roasting companies
Corso Giulio Cesare	Corso Giulio Cesare is on the outskirts of Turin, where land would have cost less
confezionamento	packaging
azioni	shares (sing: azione, f)

Useful words

The passage contains various words relating to businesses, companies and the world of work. We have added others:

un importatore	an importer (also adj: importatore, f -trice)
locali	premises (sing: locale, m)
un'impresa	an undertaking; a business, a firm
un imprenditore	an entrepreneur
una società	a company
srl (società a responsabilità limitata)	a (private) limited company
un'azienda	a company
la sede	head office
assumere	to take something on; also, to engage staff
condurre un'azienda	to run a company
la conduzione	the running
la gestione	the running, managing (of a hotel, business, etc.)
gestire	to manage
il gestore	the manager
amministratore delegato	managing director
consiglio di amministrazione	board of directors

Language points ♦

1. The present tense: use in narrative

Note how the writer uses the present tense for the steps in his story:

Luigi Lavazza <u>lascia</u> il paese
<u>Si trasferisce</u> a Torino
<u>Rileva</u> una drogheria

etc. until:

Lavazza <u>diventa</u> il caffè ufficiale della Coppa del Mondo di Calcio.

The use of the present tense when talking about the past is a common narrative device. It makes the story seem more immediate.

Reread, concentrating on picking out all these present tenses, working out or – if you need – looking up the infinitive and/or the meaning, in a dictionary.

2. Numbers, years, centuries

You will have met numbers in the early stages of learning Italian. You need them constantly when in Italy for prices, telephone numbers, time, etc. Note the following:

(*a*) In the *Text* years were written, as is usual, in figures. Remember: whether in dates or otherwise, Italians say:

1900: **millenovecento**	lit. thousand nine hundred (not nineteen hundred)
1800: **milleottocento**	lit. thousand eight hundred (not eighteen hundred)
Il teatro ha millesettecento posti a sedere	The theatre has seats for one thousand seven hundred people (not seventeen hundred)

(*b*) **Centuries: il novecento** means: 'twentieth century'. In referring to centuries from the thirteenth to the twentieth, it is usual to use the date minus the word **mille**:

il cinquecento	the sixteenth century (1500–1599)
l'ottocento	the nineteenth century (1800–1899)

However:

il ventunesimo secolo	the twenty-first century

(*c*) For a span of ten years, such as the sixties (meaning the 1960s) you say:

gli anni sessanta	the sixties
gli anni novanta	the nineties

(*d*) When numbers need to be written in words, on a cheque for instance, it is usual practice to write them as one word, no matter how long they are:

1700: **millesettecento**
1759: **millesettecentocinquantanove**

(*e*) In writing numbers, Italians use commas where we use dots (decimal points), and dots where we use commas:

1.700 (millesettecento)   1,700 (seventeen hundred)
1,7 (uno virgola sette)   1.7 (one point seven)

(*f*) The plural of **mille** is **mila** which gives:

2000: **duemila**

(*g*) When referring to a year, the word **il** is used:

il 1945 (millenovecentoquarantacinque)
il 2002 (duemiladue)

therefore:

nel millenovecentoquarantacinque   in 1945

and:

dal millenovecentoquarantacinque   since 1945

also:

Luigi Lavazza, nato a Murisengo, un paese del Monferrato alessandrino, il 24 aprile del 1859

(*h*) It is common when talking about your age, rather than giving it, to say:

Sono del '35.
I was born in 1935.

Sono del '60.
I was born in 1960.

Exercise 6

Answer in Italian, as in the example.

Example: **Quando nasce Luigi Lavazza?**
Nel milleottocentocinquantanove.

1 Quando lascia Murisengo?
2 Quando rileva la sua drogheria?
3 Qual è l'anno di nascita della Lavazza?
4 Quando si trasferisce la Lavazza in via San Tommaso?
5 Da che anno a che anno è in vigore il blocco delle importazioni ordinato da Mussolini?
6 Da quando Emilio è amministratore delegato della Lavazza?
7 Qual è l'anno di fondazione della Lavazza Premium Coffee a New York?

Language learning suggestions

Give yourself an Italian workout: work out how you might put your thoughts into Italian. Concentrate on using what you know. For instance, think out how you might introduce yourself to a new Italian colleague or to an Italian you meet while on holiday. How would you tell them about your family, colleagues, etc.? Work out how to rephrase thoughts which you don't find easy to express and how to get around any gaps in your stock of words. Talk to yourself in Italian. Make a habit of doing this with the various topics addressed in *Colloquial Italian 2* or indeed with any thoughts or ideas buzzing around in your mind, giving yourself frequent workouts. The more practice you give yourself at doing this, the easier it will become. Working out like this has been shown to be one of the most valuable aids to learning a language.

2 Di dove sei?

In this unit you will

▶ look at the use of subject pronouns (**io, tu** . . .)
▶ look at the use of informal **tu** and formal **Lei**
▶ review and practise the present tense: reflexive/reciprocal verbs
▶ consider differences between the spoken and the written language

Dialogues

Sandra interviews her friends, Marco and Beatrice, teachers in their thirties. Sylvia interviews Angelo and Lalla, a retired doctor and his wife.

Exercise 1

Listen to the recording and try to answer the questions.

1 Which speaker has one of the commonest names in Italy?
2 Which of these speakers is from a place that might be confused with Capri?
3 Which couple live outside Turin?
4 Who is from Calabria?

Dialogue 1

MARCO   Buonasera. Io mi chiamo Marco Goffi, sono insegnante di matematica e fisica, sono nato ad Avigliana e vivo e risiedo a Caprie. Entrambe queste cittadine sono vicine a Torino. E sono sposato con . . .

BEATRICE   . . . Beatrice Mezzino. Ho trentaquattro anni, sono nata a
            Torino, sono anch'io insegnante di matematica e fisica in
            un liceo dove ci sono diversi indirizzi: il classico, il linguis-
            tico, lo scientifico e l'istituto professionale per il turismo.
SANDRA   E vivete a Caprie?
BEATRICE   Viviamo a Caprie, da non confondere con Capri, che è
            tutto in un altro posto.

Lalla and Angelo

Dialogue 2

LALLA   Io mi chiamo Maria Luisa di nome ma nessuno mi conosce
            con questo nome perché fin da piccolissima mi hanno
            chiamato tutti Lalla e così rimango. E poi ho il cognome più
            comune d'Italia, che è Rossi, e quindi sono . . . se uno vuole
            prendere il mio nome 'Maria', il primo, e 'Rossi', sono la
            perfetta sconosciuta.
ANGELO   Io mi chiamo Angelo . . . null'altro da dire . . . Angelo Corica,
            ecco.
SYLVIA   Ma Lei, Signora, è proprio di qui, di Torino, vero?
LALLA   Io sono di Torino, figlia di torinesi, piemontesi da vecchia
            data.
SYLVIA   E invece Lei, dottore?
ANGELO   Io sono calabrese. Mi chiamo Angelo e sono ormai in
            pensione, ma sono stato medico fino a pochi anni fa.

Vocabulary ◆

vivo e risiedo	I live and am resident (If you live in Italy you must register your 'residence' at the local town hall. You will then be 'resident' in that 'comune' and this will appear on your identity card. See Unit 7.)
entrambe	both (m. **entrambi**)
sposato con . . . **Beatrice Mezzino**	Note: Italian women retain their own surname after marriage for legal / official purposes.
indirizzi **Maria Rossi**	courses (of study). **Indirizzo** usually means address Readers will realise Maria is the most common first name for a woman in Italy but may not know Rossi is the most common surname.
null'altro da dire	nothing else to say (Angelo simply means his name needs no comment)

Language points ◆

Subject pronouns

The subject pronouns are:

	Singular		*Plural*	
1st	**io**	I	**noi**	we
2nd	**tu**	you	**voi**	you
3rd	**lui**	he	**loro**	they (masc)
3rd	**lei**	she	**loro**	they (fem)

The pronoun is needed only for emphasis or to avoid ambiguity, as we said in Unit 1. Marco says:

Io mi chiamo Marco Goffi
My name is Marco Goffi

to make it clear he is speaking for himself. He knows his wife is going to follow him and introduce herself. An English speaker would stress the pronoun with his voice. Getting into the habit of omitting the subject pronoun is something which can make you sound much more convincingly Italian. Keep the pronoun for emphasis.

Tu / Lei

Look at whether **tu** or **Lei** was used in the two dialogues and in those in Unit 1. What can you deduce?

1 Marco and Bea are Sandra's friends – and **tu** is usually used when addressing friends and members of the family.

2 Sandra also used **tu** with Teresa and Francesca in Unit 1. People who are in the same set of circumstances – in this case Italians living in a foreign country – tend to use **tu** among themselves. Teresa is a colleague and colleagues too tend to use **tu** to each other as do members of other social groups. Tu is widely used in Italy: advertisers address their targets using **tu**.

3 Sylvia, however, used **Lei** with Lalla and Angelo. She also used the courtesy title: **dottore**. Lei is used when formality is needed: when you first meet people; in circumstances which require formality because of age differences, because of the nature of the relationship, etc. It is akin to using surnames rather than first names in English. If in doubt use **Lei**. People who feel it is inappropriate will put you right by saying:

> **Diamoci del tu, è più facile.**
> Let's use 'tu' to each other, it's easier.

4 By convention formal **Lei** is written with a capital L. In letter writing it is considered a mark of courtesy and respect. It also helps distinguish **Lei** meaning 'you' from **lei** meaning 'she', avoiding potential ambiguity. In speech the voice can usually do that although it is sometimes necessary to clarify.

Exercise 2

Various people are making introductions. The sentences are incomplete. For each blank, decide whether a personal pronoun is necessary or not. If it is, which pronoun should it be?

> Example: Marco is introducing himself and his wife, Beatrice.
> Buonasera,___io___mi chiamo Marco Goffi, mia moglie si chiama Beatrice Mezzino. ___Io___sono nato ad Avigliana,___lei___è nata a Torino.

1 Lalla is introducing herself and her husband, Angelo.
_____ mi chiamo Maria Luisa, mio marito si chiama Angelo. _____ sono nata e cresciuta in Piemonte, a Torino. _____ è nato e cresciuto in Calabria.

2 Teresa introduces herself and friend, Francesca.

_____ mi chiamo Teresa, la mia amica si chiama Francesca.
_____ siamo tutt'e due italiane, ma _____ sono di Napoli,
_____ è di Padova.

3 Francesca is talking to Teresa.

Francesca: _____ sono di Padova, _____ di dove sei?
Teresa: _____ sono di Napoli, e _____ vivo in
Inghilterra da alcuni anni. _____ da quanto tempo
vivi in Inghilterra?
Francesca: _____ sono arrivata in Inghilterra pochi
mesi fa.

4 Sylvia is talking to Angelo.

Sylvia: Dottore, _____ è di Torino?
Dott. Corica: No, mia moglie è di Torino, _____ sono
calabrese. E _____, signora, di dove è?
Sylvia: _____ sono inglese. _____ sono nata e cresciuta
in Inghilterra.

Exercise 3

Make sentences using the information given:

Example: Franco introduces himself and his wife, Antonella.
(**Franco: milanese, pensionato, 60 anni, sposato con
Antonella: veneta, 50 anni, impiegata.**)

**Io mi chiamo Franco, sono milanese, ho 60 anni e
sono pensionato. Mia moglie si chiama Antonella.
(Lei) è veneta, ha 50 anni ed è impiegata.**

1 Giovanna introduces herself and her sister, Paola.
(Giovanna: casalinga, sposata, 55 anni, nata a Bari; Paola: avvocato, single, 45 anni, nata a Napoli.)

2 Enrico introduces himself and his brother, Marco.
(Enrico: 21 anni, studente di medicina, residente in Italia; Marco:
26 anni, giornalista, residente in Inghilterra.)

Antonio Ricci © *La Stampa*

Text ꞏ))👂

The newspaper La Stampa, *runs a regular feature in which well-known Italians are interviewed. Here is part of the interview with Antonio Ricci, creator of the popular television programme:* Striscia la notizia *which might be translated: 'The comic strip news'. (Striscia: comic strip. Strisciante also means 'crafty', 'sneaky', so the idea of undermining, making fun of the news is also there.) It goes out nightly after the main news bulletin on Canale 5.*

Exercise 4

Before you read the text, look at the questions. Then read the text and try to answer.

1 Where does Antonio Ricci work?
2 Can you find any information about a typical working day for him?
3 What does he tell you about his reading of the newspapers?
4 Where is his home? What does he say about the place?
5 What is his attitude towards money?
6 Ricci is, as we have said, the creator of a satirical, humorous TV programme. Do you see any signs of his humour in what he says?

La mia vita è come un bar: mi interessa solo il divertimento

Antonio Ricci è nato ad Albenga (in provincia di Savona) il 26 giugno 1950. Ex docente di scuola media, ex autore di cabaret, è stato autore di programmi tv come 'Drive-in'. Dal 1988 è la mente di 'Striscia la notizia', programma di grande successo, in onda dopo il tg su Canale 5.

DOMANDA

Antonio Ricci, lei è l'ideatore di 'Striscia la notizia'. Come ama definirsi?

ANTONIO RICCI

Senz'altro autore, di cosa non so. E' un termine ampio, perché uno può essere anche autore di una rapina.

DOMANDA

Come si svolge la sua giornata?

ANTONIO RICCI

Comincia presto, per un problema tecnico. Nella stanza del residence dove vivo a Milano 2, nei mesi in cui lavoro, non ci sono le persiane e c'è una tenda che non chiude bene. Alle sette di mattina filtra la luce e io mi sveglio, anche se sono andato a dormire alle cinque.

DOMANDA

Guarda molto la televisione?

ANTONIO RICCI

Sì, al mattino presto. Seguo il televideo, i telegiornali, pezzetti di 'Costanzo show'. Dopo vado in ufficio e comincio a leggere i giornali, anzi prima faccio colazione al bar con un caffè e due brioches zuccherate.

DOMANDA

Quanti giornali legge, che cosa le interessa?

ANTONIO RICCI

Li sfoglio, non li leggo attentamente. Salto lo sport che non mi interessa affatto.

DOMANDA

A che ora sono pronti i testi di 'Striscia'?

ANTONIO RICCI

Verso le 19, con la possibilità di cambiamenti che a volte avvengono quando siamo già in onda. E' una trasmissione molto preparata ma che ha il sapore di 'improvvisata'.

DOMANDA	Lei vive ad Alassio. Come si sta in una cittadina di provincia?
ANTONIO RICCI	Molto bene, si respira aria buona, si guarda il mare, si sta con gli amici.
DOMANDA	Lei è parsimonioso?
ANTONIO RICCI	No, io scialacquo, ma senza esagerare.
DOMANDA	Cioè?
ANTONIO RICCI	So che posso vivere mangiando un pomodoro. Al di là del pomodoro tutto è prostituzione. Però tutto il resto che arriva io me lo godo senza impazzire, coi piedi per terra, sapendo che è una cosa che può finire e che è dovuta a una serie di congiunzioni astrali particolarmente fortunate.

Adapted from: *La Stampa*, 26 October 2000

Vocabulary ♦

Albenga, Savona	towns in Liguria
in onda	on air (lit. **onda** = wave, **in onda** = on the air waves)
senz'altro	(here) definitely, certainly, of course
docente	teacher
tg	**telegiornale**, tv news
residence	apartment block (containing usually small furnished apartments with cooking facilities, sometimes fully serviced)
Milano 2	residential area in the outskirts of Milan, built in the 1970s as an 'ideal' place to live
'Costanzo show'	a popular, long-running TV chat show, also on Canale 5 – its presenter is Maurizio Costanzo
televideo	teletext
anzi	or rather (can also mean 'on the contrary')
Alassio	a resort on the coast of Liguria
scialacquo	I spend lavishly

Language points ♦

1. Spoken/written language

Compare this interview with those at the start of the unit and in Unit 1. This purports to be an interview but it lacks the authentic spoken-language characteristics of the earlier interviews. Notice how Francesca, for instance, hesitates, then changes direction as she explains about the frequency of Slav-sounding names in the frontier area. And Lalla, too, as she explains that she has probably the most common name in Italy: Maria Rossi. Antonio Ricci on the other hand does not hesitate, his sentences are well formed and, although lively, slightly unnatural as speech.

Use the hesitant nature of normal speech to your advantage. If you feel you can't cope with the sentence the way you have begun it, start again, express your meaning differently. We do this as we speak our own language, it's absolutely normal.

2. Reflexive verbs – revision

Several of the interviewees use reflexive verbs. Reflexive verbs are verbs of all types (-are, -ere, -ire), regular and irregular, used with a reflexive pronoun to express a particular meaning. **Svegliare qualcuno** is 'to wake someone up'. **Svegliarsi** is 'to wake up', as in: 'I wake up every morning tired', literally: 'to wake oneself'. Some English verbs work that way too: 'to enjoy oneself' (**divertirsi**), 'I enjoy myself' (**mi diverto**), 'you enjoy yourself' (**ti diverti**), etc. But verbs which are reflexive in English are not necessarily reflexive in Italian.

In the infinitive, *the reflexive pronoun follows the verb*:

vestirsi – to get dressed (-**si** is the reflexive pronoun)

In the finite forms, *the reflexive pronoun precedes the verb* and changes according to the subject. (A finite form is a form which shows person and tense, as opposed, for example, to the infinitive.) Here is a model.

Singular

1	**mi**	**vesto**	I get dressed	lit. I dress myself
2	**ti**	**vesti**	you get dressed	lit. you dress yourself
3	**si**	**veste**	he / she / it gets dressed	lit. he/she/it dresses himself/herself/itself

Plural

1	ci	**vestiamo**	we get dressed	lit. we dress ourselves
2	vi	**vestite**	you get dressed	lit. you dress yourselves
3	si	**vestono**	they get dressed	lit. they dress themselves

3. Reciprocal verbs

These are similar and should not cause difficulty. The reciprocal pronoun has the same form as the reflexive pronoun and corresponds to 'each other'. Reciprocal verbs are used in the plural only since at least two people are involved.

Vi conoscete?
Do you know each other?

Ci conosciamo da più di vent'anni.
We have known each other for more than 20 years.

Ci vediamo almeno una volta alla settimana.
We see each other at least once a week.

Si telefonano ogni giorno.
They telephone each other every day.

Arrivederci.
lit. until we see each other again (a + rivederci).

4. Special use of the reflexive

Note: many verbs which are not normally used reflexively are made reflexive to express the pleasure derived from an action.

Ecco, ho finito. Adesso mi faccio una tazza di tè.
There, I've finished. Now I'll make a nice cup of tea.

Adesso mi leggo il giornale.
Now I am going enjoy a read of the paper.

In fact Ricci uses something similar when talking about money: **me lo godo**, **lo** being **il resto**. Look back and see.

Careful! Talking about Alassio and answering the question: **Come si sta?** Ricci uses: **si respira, si guarda**. This **si** is not a reflexive pronoun, it is impersonal, i.e. 'one'. We will look at the impersonal form of verbs in Unit 9.

Exercise 5

In this exercise you are going to use some reflexive verbs expressing common actions in our daily routine.

a This is what Antonio Ricci does every day. The verbs for the actions have been supplied in brackets, but you need to put them into the correct form, as shown in the example.

Antonio Ricci (svegliarsi) <u>si sveglia</u> molto presto la mattina. Poi (alzarsi) _____ , (lavarsi) _____ , (vestirsi) _____ , (farsi) _____ il caffè e guarda il telegiornale. La sera, torna a casa molto tardi. (Togliersi) _____ le scarpe, (svestirsi) _____ , (farsi) _____ una doccia, (mettersi) _____ il pigiama. Poi (coricarsi) _____ e (addormentarsi) _____ .

b Now rewrite the paragraph above in the first person, as if Antonio Ricci himself were speaking. There is an example to start you off.

<u>Mi sveglio</u> molto presto la mattina . . .

Exercise 6

More reflexive verbs, these used to express feelings and states of mind, moods:

annoiarsi, divertirsi, arrabbiarsi, rallegrarsi, innervosirsi, stupirsi, entusiasmarsi

Match the phrase on the left with its other half, the phrase in the right-hand column which best seems to complete it. Then put the verb in the first column into the correct form.

Example: **1. si annoiano – g.**
Gli studenti di solito si annoiano se le lezioni dei loro professori non sono interessanti.

1 Gli studenti di solito (annoiarsi) _____	a	. . . quando la sua squadra preferita vince la partita.
2 I bambini di solito (divertirsi) _____	b	. . . che Anna e Marco si erano lasciati?

3 Mio figlio è appassionato c ... quando non riesco a
di calcio, e di solito   dormire perché il mio vicino di
(arrabbiarsi) _____   casa ascolta la musica a volume
                                 troppo alto.

4 Noi genitori di solito   d ... se la sua squadra perde
(rallegrarsi) _____   una partita.

5 Di solito (io – innervosirsi) e ... quando vediamo che i
_____   nostri figli sono felici.

6 Mio marito di solito   f ... quando possono giocare
(entusiasmarsi) _____   con i loro coetanei.

7 Perché (tu – stupirsi)   g ... se le lezioni dei loro
_____ ? Non lo sapevi   professori non sono interessanti.

Language learning suggestions

Be aware that different people learn in different ways. You need to try to find ways that work for you. It may be that listening to the tapes frequently fixes pieces of Italian in your mind. On the other hand you may be a person who likes to set things out in tables, look for patterns, perhaps chant verbs to yourself. There is no right or wrong way. Just your way.

3 Che tipo sei?

Padova

Siena

Catania

In this unit you will

▶ consider how to describe yourself and others
▶ revise the use of the possessive adjective with members of the family (mother, father, etc.)
▶ revise **avere/essere** and parts of the body
▶ revise the pronouns **ci** and **vi**
▶ consider suffixes
▶ look at unstressed object pronouns
▶ revisit the present tense of irregular verbs

Dialogue

Listen to Tiziana describing herself and her family to Sandra. Then answer some questions. Tiziana is from Sicily which, being centrally situated in the Mediterranean, has suffered many foreign invasions throughout its history, including the ancient Greeks, north African peoples, the Normans and the Spanish.

Exercise 1

1 How many brothers does Tiziana have?
2 What facial feature does she share with her father?
3 What particular aspects of her mother's appearance give her an Indian look?

Tiziana

TIZIANA	Allora, io sono Tiziana e vengo da Catania, quindi sono siciliana.
SANDRA	Raccontami della tua famiglia.
TIZIANA	Allora, siamo in sei: i miei genitori, i miei tre fratelli, un maschio e due femmine.
SANDRA	E se tu dovessi descrivere i tuoi fratelli e sorelle . . . fisicamente?
TIZIANA	Ma, fisicamente siamo delle fotocopie, che cosa strana! Perché secondo me anche i miei genitori si assomigliano in qualche modo . . . gli occhi, l'espressione . . . naso e labbra sono un po' diversi, ma l'espressione è la stessa. E hanno tutti e due gli occhi castani abbastanza grandi . . . E i figli sono un miscuglio . . . non possiamo dire che assomigliamo a mamma o a papà, ma assomigliamo a tutti e due. Papà c'ha un nasone, e io l'ho preso da lui! La mamma . . . la mamma ha un aspetto devo dire un po' indianeggiante, cioè . . . le labbra carnose, il naso dritto, occhioni neri, e capelli neri lucenti . . . proprio indiano, potrei dire . . .
SANDRA	Chissà cos'è . . . forse c'è qualcosa di arabo?
TIZIANA	Sì, il fatto che siamo stati dominati dagli arabi per parecchio tempo . . . sì, sicuramente . . . noi siamo un crocevia, sono passate tutte le popolazioni antiche, e quindi sì, siamo un miscuglio di colori, trovi dal biondo con la carne chiarissima, allo scuro con gli occhi neri.

Vocabulary ◆

siamo in sei	there are six of us
siamo in due	there are two of us
assomigliare	to resemble, look like (**assomigliare a qualcuno**)
assomigliarsi	to look like each other
nasone	a big nose (-**one** (f. -**ona**) is a suffix, adding an idea of largeness)
indianeggiante	Indian-looking (the suffix -**eggiante** conveys the idea: looking like, behaving like)
carnagione	complexion

Exercise 2

Try writing down the words for the main features of a face (e.g. **occhi**) and then, for each one, list as many related nouns and adjectives as possibile (e.g. for **occhi: azzurri**). Then look at the nouns and adjectives relating to facial appearance in the box.

Bocca:	piccola, grande, ben disegnata, sensuale, una boccuccia
Capelli:	scuri, chiari, neri, bruni, castani, biondi, grigi, brizzolati, lisci, ondulati, ricci, sottili, delicati, morbidi, lunghi, corti, a spazzola, sciolti, legati, lucidi, opachi, crespi
Carnagione:	chiara, scura, mediterranea, fresca, giovane
Labbra:	carnose, sottili, rosse, screpolate
Naso:	dritto, all'insù, camuso, greco, lungo, a patata, un nasino, un nasone
Occhi:	piccoli, grandi, a mandorla, allungati, chiari, scuri, verdi, marroni, azzurri, profondi, intensi, espressivi, inespressivi, acquosi, freddi, tristi, sorridenti, allegri, maligni, spiritosi, inquieti, strabici, degli occhioni, degli occhietti
Orecchie:	a punta, ben disegnate, a sventola, piccole

We wouldn't expect you to have produced even half the words in this list, but offer them so that you can extend the number and range of the words at your disposal.

Language points ◆

1. *La tua famiglia, i miei genitori.* Possessive adjectives

The possessive adjective in Italian is usually preceded by the article, for example:

il mio lavoro	my work
la mia amica	my friend
i miei amici	my friends
le mie sorelle	my sisters

The definite article is not used with words for family members, in the singular and unqualified, i.e. without an accompanying adjective. So:

mio padre   my father
mia zia   my aunt

but:

il mio fratello giovane
my young brother

This exception does not apply to **loro**:

il loro fratello   their brother

It is usual to refer to **la mamma** ('my mother'), **il papà, la nonna, il nonno,** and even **lo zio, la zia** with the article and without a possessive adjective, when the meaning is 'my'. Also **il babbo**, a Tuscan/Sardinian word but now used quite widely.

Note also: **i miei, i tuoi, i suoi,** meaning 'my, your, his / her parents'.

2. *Avere / essere* and parts of the body

Notice that Tiziana uses **avere** + the article:

<u>**hanno**</u> tutti e due <u>**gli occhi castani**</u>

In English this may be translated as:

They both have brown eyes or Their eyes are brown.

This second structure would be unusual in Italian (although grammatically correct). It is usual to use **avere** and the definite article rather than **essere** with a possessive.

Ho i capelli biondi, ho gli occhi verdi.
My hair is fair, my eyes are green.

Rather than:

I miei capelli sono biondi, i miei occhi sono verdi.

3. *Papà c'ha un nasone.* The pronouns *ci* and *vi*

(*a*) It is common in spoken Italian to insert **ci** before parts of the verb **avere**. **C'ha** is pronounced: **cià**.

However, to use **ci** as the subject of **essere** is standard Italian. Antonio Ricci says of his apartment:

non *ci sono* le persiane e *c'è* una tenda che non chiude bene
there are no shutters and there is a curtain which doesn't close properly

Ci can also be the subject of **vuole / vogliono:**

Ci vogliono tre ore per andare a Roma in treno.
It takes three hours to go to Rome by train.

Ci vuole un'ora per andare a Palermo in autobus.
It takes an hour to go to Palermo by bus.

Vi cannot be substituted for **ci** in this expression.

(*b*) **Ci** can be an object pronoun to replace a noun, a pronoun or a phrase:

quando _ci_ ripenso
when I think <u>about it</u> again

(NB: **pensare _a_ qualcosa**   to think <u>about</u> something)

Ogni quanto vai a Roma? _Ci_ vado una volta al mese.
How often do you go to Rome? I go <u>there</u> once a month.

In rather literary Italian, **vi** is sometimes used rather than **ci**. If you plan to read Italian, you may meet it:

La Galleria degli Uffizi è uno dei musei più importanti del mondo. _Vi_ sono conservati molti oggetti d'arte.

The Uffizi Gallery is one of the most important museums in the world. Many works of art are kept there.

Exercise 3

Chiara and Francesca are describing their respective cities. Insert into the blank spaces the expressions given in the box above the description. Be careful: the expressions are not in order and can be used more than once. In each box the first sentence is completed as an example.

> ci sono   ci vuole   c'è

Che tipo di vita si fa a Siena?
Si fa la vita di una città di provincia. <u>C'è</u> un teatro, si va a teatro. _____ una famosa accademia musicale, l'Accademia

Chigiana, e quindi _____ la possibilità di andare a concerti.
E' una città molto tranquilla, per cui dopo cena puoi uscire a
passeggio, non _____ pericoli. E poi _____ molto turismo,
_____ l'Università, e _____ una banca importante, il Monte
dei Paschi di Siena.

Purtroppo Siena è molto isolata. Per andare a Firenze in treno
_____ molto tempo. E quando _____ stata la possibilità di
aprire un aeroporto, i senesi hanno detto: 'Ma noi stiamo bene
così!' _____ una chiusura notevole al mondo esterno.

c'è   ci sono

Padova che tipo di città è?
Padova è una città di media grandezza. E' estremamente
vivibile, è a misura d'uomo. E' una città universitaria con 60
mila studenti, quindi <u>ci sono</u> tantissimi giovani da tutta Italia,
e _____ molta varietà.

_____ un'isola pedonale al centro della città dove tu puoi
andare a passeggiare, dove sai che non _____ macchine, dove
_____ anche la sede dell'antica Università, che è il ritrovo dei
giovani.

E' una città piacevole, culturalmente è molto viva, _____ molte
offerte, tantissimi corsi, conferenze, biblioteche, librerie. _____
tanti centri sportivi. E' molto viva, _____ continuamente molte
idee . . .

Note: **Si fa la vita di una città di provincia.** 'One lives the life of a
provincial town.' (**Si** again used to mean 'one'. See Unit 9.)

4. Suffixes

Suffixes are elements which can be added to a word to make a new
word with a different meaning. There are broadly two types of suffix:

(*a*) Those which change one type of word to another, e.g.:

* verb to adjective: **mangiare – mangiabile; leggere – leggibile**
* or adjective to noun: **bello – bellezza**
* or adjective to adverb: **lento – lentamente**.

(b) Those which modify the meaning of the word without changing its function. In this chapter, we are going to consider this second type.

In Tiziana's interview you met:

-one:	naso	nose
	nasone	big nose (both nouns)
-eggiante:	indiano	Indian
	indianeggiante	Indian looking (both adjectives)

In the word list you met:

-uccia:	bocca	mouth
	boccuccia	pretty little mouth (both nouns)
-etti:	occhi	eyes
	occhietti	small eyes (both nouns)
-oni:	occhioni	large eyes

You will also be familiar with some such as:

-issimo:	bello	beautiful
	bellissimo	very beautiful (both adjectives)
-ino:	fratello	brother
	fratellino	little brother (both nouns)

All these suffixes are added to nouns and adjectives to convey judgments or views on size, affection and esteem or lack of it.

Smallness:	-ino, -etto, -ello
Largeness:	-one (NB feminine: -ona)
Affection:	-uccio, but also -ino, -ello
Disdain, contempt:	-accio
-ish:	-astro (**giallo, giallastro**)
	Note: **fratellastro, sorellastra**
	half-brother, half-sister. Also: -iccio
	(**malato, malaticcio** ill, under the weather)

However, there are subtle shades of meaning (**sfumature**); for instance, -uccio can also express contempt, as can -iccio.

Because of the wide variety of these suffixes and the subtle differences of meaning involved, you are advised to learn them as you meet them. It takes time to master them. You are advised to note what Italians say and imitate them. Gradually you will feel able to use them more freely and even use them as creatively as Italians do.

Exercise 4

Add suffixes to the words listed to change the meaning, as in the example:

naso nose; **nasone** a big nose; **nasino** a small nose

occhi: big eyes, small eyes, nasty eyes
mani: big hands, small hands, rough hands
denti: big teeth, small teeth
piedi: big feet, small feet

Text

Specchio is a glossy weekly magazine published by the newspaper *La Stampa. The passage which follows is a letter published in the 'agony column'.*

Exercise 5

Say whether the following statements are true or false:

1 Federica thinks her biggest weakness is that she doesn't listen to other people.
2 Federica has a good opinion of herself and is particularly proud of being shapely.
3 Federica thinks that 'he' is very handsome.
4 Federica thinks her rival is intelligent.

Mi chiamo Federica e ho 17 anni e le mie idee sono piuttosto anticonformiste per la verità. Ascolto musica punk e anche gente come Bob Dylan, Joan Baez, i Doors e gli Who. Leggo un sacco di libri, tutto quel che mi capita. Ho un sacco di difetti, ma so ascoltare. Ho un bel viso, ma odio il mio fisico in stile Sabrina Ferilli che è un gran problema quando compro un vestito: in un mondo di anoressiche è incredibilmente difficile, per chi porta una quarta di reggiseno, trovare una maglietta qualsiasi!

Veniamo a lui. Uno di quelli che vestono scarpe Prada, pantaloni Gucci, . . . Bello come il sole: occhi grigi, che passano dalla gradazione ghiaccio a quella asfalto in un attimo. Mani bellissime e un corpo stupendo. Forse il paragone è un po' azzardato, ma sembra il David di Michelangelo. Lui razionale e timido. Io passionale e solare. Capirai che due persone più diverse non potrebbero esistere.

(*Lui le fa la corte, escono insieme per un breve periodo, poi lei scopre che lui aveva già un'altra ragazza.*)

Un giorno scopro che lui ha la fidanzata da nove mesi (perciò anche quando mi ha baciata, fingeva). Una ragazza insignificante. Oca. Un'idiota sotto tutti gli aspetti. Non parlo per gelosia, lo dicono tutti. Sono infelice. Lui mi descrive come il suo ideale di donna: alta, formosa, sorridente, dolce, femminile e sexy. La sua attuale ragazza è bassa, piatta, rude e sboccata.

Non ci capisco più niente, sai? Cosa pensi di lui? Mi ama? Avremo mai un futuro insieme?

Chicca

Adapted from: Cuori allo Specchio, edited by Massimo Gramellini, in *Specchio*, weekly supplement to *La Stampa*, 30 March 2002, n. 319

Vocabulary ◆

The style is that of a teenager!

tutto quel che mi capita	everything that comes my way
ho un sacco di difetti	I've got loads of faults (lit. a bag of . . .; **un sacco di** – very common way to say: **molti**)
il mio fisico in stile Sabrina Ferilli	Sabrina Ferilli is a film and TV actress, who fits the standard idea of an Italian beauty: dark hair, shapely, curvaceous, etc.
chi porta una quarta di reggiseno	those who wear D-cup bras
oca	lit. goose (used here of a woman, who lacks both intelligence and education)
formosa	shapely, of generous proportions
piatta	flat-chested

rude	coarse (not: impolite. A word that looks like an English word but in fact has a different meaning from its look-alike is often referred to as a 'false friend' because it is misleading rather than helpful)
sboccata	vulgar, loudmouthed

Exercise 6

This a list of adjectives used to describe what people look like.

> aggraziato brutto in forma sgraziato alto effeminato
> magro slanciato asciutto fuori forma mascolino
> snello atletico goffo mingherlino sottile attraente
> grasso muscoloso tarchiato basso imponente
> robusto bello in carne sexy

Arrange them in various ways:

1 Pairs of opposites.
2 Those which describe you – and those which refer to characteristics you would not want attributed to you.

Language points ♦

More pronouns

(For a Table of Pronouns, see the Grammar reference).

(*a*) **mi, ti, ci, vi**

Mi is the object pronoun for **io,** meaning 'me', 'to me', 'for me'. An object is the person, or the thing, that receives the action of the verb (see also Unit 5). Federica says:

Lui <u>mi</u> descrive come il suo ideale di donna.
He describes <u>me</u> as his ideal for a woman.

tutto quel che <u>mi</u> capita
everything which comes <u>to me</u> (comes my way)

Similarly **ti** – 'you' (singular), 'to you', 'for you':

<u>Ti</u> amo così come sei.
I love <u>you</u> the way you are.

Questa maglia non ti sta bene: è troppo piccola <u>per te</u>.
This top doesn't suit you: is too small <u>for you</u>.

Ci: 'us', 'to us', 'for us':

La mamma <u>ci</u> chiama, ragazzi.
Mum's calling <u>us</u>, guys.

I nonni <u>ci</u> hanno detto che vogliono andare a Parigi.
The grandparents told <u>us</u> that they want to go to Paris.

Vi: 'you', 'to you', 'for you' (plural):

Se venite a trovarmi, <u>vi</u> vedrò con piacere!
If you come to see me, I shall be pleased to see <u>you</u>.

Se avete bisogno di un passaggio, <u>vi</u> porto alla stazione.
If you need a lift, I will take <u>you</u> to the station.

Note: All these object pronouns go directly in front of the verbs. They cannot stand alone. Nor do they normally follow the verb.

(b) lo, la, li, le; gli, le, gli / loro

In dealing with **ci, vi, mi, ti,** we did not deal with whether they were direct or indirect objects of the verb since these pronouns can be either. In using the pronouns for the third persons, singular and plural, it is essential to distinguish. To distinguish direct from indirect objects, the verb is the key.

The verb **conoscere** takes (i.e. works with) a direct object, i.e. there is no preposition between the verb and its object. The object is direct, e.g.:

Conosco una ragazza italiana.
I know an Italian girl.

Conosco tre lingue.
I know three languages.

The verb **parlare** needs a preposition before the object. The object is indirect, e.g.:

Parlo <u>a</u> Francesca <u>delle</u> vacanze.
I am talking <u>to</u> Francesca <u>about</u> my holidays.

(i) **lo, la, li, le,** are the direct object pronouns corresponding to the 3rd person.

> <u>Lo</u> dicono tutti.
> Everybody says <u>it</u>.

(ii) **gli, le, gli/loro** are the indirect object pronouns for the third person.

> Lui <u>le</u> fa la corte.
> He pays court <u>to her</u>.

Note: the direct object pronouns **lo, la, li, le,** and the indirect object pronouns **gli** and **le** also precede the verb and cannot stand alone or follow the verb.

The plural 'to them' is in careful Italian **loro,** which is placed after the verb. There is a strong tendency in spoken Italian to use **gli** instead. **Gli** must precede the verb.

> <u>Gli</u> parlo delle mie vacanze / parlo <u>loro</u> delle mie vacanze.
> I am talking <u>to them</u> about my holidays.

Pronouns with more than one function

Reading this carefully, you will become aware, if you did not already know, that some words have more than one function. For instance, **lui** can be subject pronoun 'he'; and stressed pronoun which will in English be 'he' or 'him', depending on the grammar of the use. Try not to worry about this. It gradually falls into place. The overall picture can be seen in the table in the Grammar reference.

Irregular verbs, present tense

Exercise 7

Federica uses some very common irregular verbs. Reread the letter and pick out irregular verbs used in the present tense, then check your answer with the Key to exercises.

Irregular verbs tend to be commonly used verbs and in some ways this makes them easy to learn, since you meet them so often that you become familiar with them almost without effort. As with the present tense of regular verbs, the endings are often easy:

1st pers. sing.	always ends in -o
2nd pers. sing.	always ends in -i
1st pers. plur.	always ends in -iamo

The problem lies in the first part of the verb, often called 'the root'. For many people it helps to group verbs. We have set out a suggested grouping in the Grammar reference. Look at it and you will see that, for instance, **potere, sapere, volere** have similarities in form: many learners find it helpful to learn them as a group.

Language learning suggestions

This is a tip for learning irregular verbs. Below is a chart divided into rectangles. Each rectangle contains the infinitive of an irregular verb. Photocopy and enlarge the chart and cut the copy along the lines, so that you have a set of rectangular pieces of paper, each with the infinitive of a verb written on it. Then you take a rectangle out at random and test yourself on that verb. You may want to write the correct form on the back so that you can check. Carry them with you and, in odd moments, as you wait for a bus or at the dentist's, work on three or four. 'Little and often' is a good motto for language study and this is a way of putting it into practice, so that even very short idle moments are used productively.

andare	dare	fare	stare
sapere	tenere	venire	comporre
rimanere	salire	scegliere	valere
dovere	potere	volere	bere
sedere	uscire	dire	trarre
ottenere	convenire	supporre	assalire
togliere	sciogliere	possedere	riuscire
trasalire	togliere	equivalere	prevalere

4 Che cosa pensi di me?

• Modena

• Catania

In this unit you will

▶ consider how to describe character
▶ look at another object pronoun, **ne**, and at combining pronouns
▶ revise the present subjunctive
▶ meet some aids to guessing new words
▶ revise asking questions

Dialogue

Sandra asks Tiziana to describe herself. The day before their conversation, Tiziana had been wondering how much one can deduce about people from watching the way they walk. Her thoughts start there.

Exercise 1

1 What does Tiziana's husband think her way of walking indicates?
2 What does Tiziana think makes her slim?
3 What does she hope people see in her expression?

TIZIANA   Mmm ... ieri parlavo proprio di questo, chiedevo a mio marito: 'Ma che cosa te ne pare?' Fa: 'Mi dà l'impressione che quando cammini, tu, cammini per un obiettivo'. E quindi il mio fisico secondo me risente di questo. Infatti è nervoso ... anche se non faccio sport da parecchio tempo, piuttosto ... teso ...

SANDRA   Tonico!

TIZIANA   ... tonico, proprio per il fatto che cammino e corro sempre, da una parte all'altra, solitamente della città, anche della casa! E quindi mi ritrovo ad essere snella ... ma non eccessivamente, sono una falsa magra. La gente pensa che io sia più magra di quanto in realtà non sono. E poi credo di avere un viso che esprime quello che in realtà io sono, in qualche modo. Cioè io mi trovo ad essere aperta con la gente ... spero che la gente mi veda in questa maniera. Almeno, credo che i miei occhi diano l'impressione che comunque voglio cercare sempre qualcosa, comunque disponibile a dare, comunicativa.

Vocabulary ♦

fa	he said (spoken language), lit. he does/makes (from **fare**)
infatti	indeed, really (**infatti** is a 'false friend', and doesn't mean the same as English: in fact, which is **in realtà** – see below)
tonico	Refers to muscle tone. Tiziana describes her physique as 'tense'. Sandra is putting it positively, perhaps: fit
falsa magra	Said of someone who looks slim/thin but isn't really
in realtà	actually, in fact (note that Italian **attualmente** is another 'false friend' and means: at the present (time), nowadays)

Language points ♦

1. The pronoun *ne*

Tiziana says to her husband:

Ma che cosa te ne pare?
What do you think <u>about it</u>? (The expression she uses can't be translated literally.)

Ne is used to replace **di** + a noun, a pronoun, a phrase (in this case: **del mio modo di camminare**).

Quante mele hai comprato? <u>Ne</u> ho comprate cinque. (ne = di mele)
How many apples did you buy? I bought five (<u>of them</u>).

Quanti fratelli hai? <u>Ne</u> ho due. (ne = di fratelli)
How many brothers do you have? I have two (<u>of them</u>).

Mi piace questa gonna, ma mi sembra piccola. Tu, cosa <u>ne</u> pensi?
(ne = della <u>gonna</u>)
I like this skirt, but it looks small. What do you think (<u>about it</u>)?

Quanti anni hai? Ne ho 21. (ne = di anni)
How old are you? I am 21.

Exercise 2

Answer the question using the information given in brackets.

    Example: **Quanti anni hai? (30)**
               Ne ho trenta.

1 Quanti figli hai? (3)
2 Quante sorelle hai? (13)
3 Quanti fratelli hai? (15)
4 Quanti gatti hai? (7)
5 Quante paia di scarpe hai? (53)
6 Quanti ombrelli hai? (23)

2. Combined pronouns

When two pronouns are combined, the first is modified so that: **mi, ti, ci, vi,** become **me, te, ce, ve.** This also applies to **si**, the reflexive pronoun, which becomes **se. Gli** and **le** become **glie** and in writing are joined to **lo, la, li, le** and **ne.**

    Hence: **Che cosa te ne pare?**

The order is fixed:

(i)   **me, te, glie, se, ce, ve** come first;
(ii) **lo, la, li, le, ne** come second.

Most learners will find this difficult to absorb in this analytic, concentrated form. It is here for reference. In our experience the way to learn this is to listen / look out for and imitate examples. For reference there is a complete table of pronouns in the Grammar reference.

3. The present subjunctive

Talking about herself, Tiziana is diffident and so expresses herself less categorically than when she was talking about her family. She says:

    Credo di avere un viso che esprime . . .
    I think I have a face that expresses . . .

rather than:

> **Ho un viso che esprime ...**
> I have a face that expresses ...

and:

> **Spero che la gente mi veda in questa maniera.**
> I hope people see me in this way.

> **Credo che i miei occhi diano l'impressione ...**
> I think my eyes give the impression that ...

> **La gente pensa che io sia più magra di quanto in realtà non sono.**
> People think I'm thinner than in fact I am.

The use of **pensare, credere, sperare** requires her to use the present subjunctive: **veda, diano, sia.** We explain this after the section, below, on the form of the present subjunctive.

Sandra also uses the subjunctive, but the imperfect (**dovessi**), when she says:

> **E se tu dovessi descrivere i tuoi fratelli?**
> And if you had to describe your brothers?

(For the imperfect subjunctive, see Unit 11.)

Form

- All three persons of the singular have the same ending:

    -i for verbs in the first group;
    -a for all other verbs.

- The first person plural for all verbs is:

    -iamo as in the present indicative.

- The second person plural for all verbs is:

    -iate.

Regular verbs form the present subjunctive by adding the endings to the stem of the first person singular of the present indicative. The verb groups split into two types: 1. -are verbs and 2. the rest.

Note: verbs like **finire** have -isc- in the same parts as in the present tense.

Present subjunctive of regular verbs

	-are verbs	parlare	-ere and -ire verbs	decidere	finire
1st sing	- i	parli	-a	decida	finisca
2nd sing	- i	parli	-a	decida	finisca
3rd sing	- i	parli	-a	decida	finisca
1st plur	-iamo	parliamo	-iamo	decidiamo	finiamo
2nd plur	-iate	parliate	-iate	decidiate	finiate
3rd plur	-ino	parlino	-ano	decidano	finiscano

Note: Since the form of the subjunctive is the same for all three persons in the singular, you often need to use the personal pronouns (io, tu, lui, lei) to avoid confusion.

Note: The vowel printed in italics is to draw your attention to the irregular stress in the third person plural.

Irregular present subjunctive

Verbs which are irregular in the present indicative are also irregular in the present subjunctive. Some form the present subjunctive by adding the *2nd / 3rd group endings* to the stem of the *first person plural* of the present indicative, e.g.:

	endings	essere (s-/si-)	avere (abb-/abbi-)	fare (facc-/facci-)	dare (d-/di-)
1st sing	-a	sia	abbia	faccia	dia
2nd sing	-a	sia	abbia	faccia	dia
3rd sing	-a	sia	abbia	faccia	dia
1st plur	-iamo	siamo	abbiamo	facciamo	diamo
2nd plur	-iate	siate	abbiate	facciate	diate
3rd plur	-ano	siano	abbiano	facciano	diano

Other verbs which do this are: sapere (sappia), volere (voglia), dire (dica).

For the other irregular verbs, refer to the Grammar reference at the end of the book.

Exercise 3

You have organised a blind date (**appuntamento al buio**) for Marta and Gianni who you think are well suited to each other. Use the information below to write down what each hopes before the meeting.

Example: **Marta spera che Gianni**
avere i capelli biondi.
Marta spera che Gianni abbia i capelli biondi.

Marta spera che Gianni

1 non **amare** il calcio.
2 non **essere** vegetariano.
3 **essere** appassionato di musica latino-americana e **sapere** suonare la chitarra.

Gianni spera che Marta

4 **essere** bruna.
5 **avere** la voce dolce.
6 **amare** viaggiare.
7 **adorare** i ristoranti di pesce.

Use

Remember: the subjunctive is not a tense: it is a 'mood' or 'mode' and it has four tenses: present, past, imperfect and pluperfect. In this unit we are looking at the present tense only.

The *tense* of a verb tells us when a certain action is taking, has taken or will take place. Present, future, imperfect, perfect, etc. are tenses.

The *mood* of a verb reflects the attitude of the speaker towards the action or state he is expressing. The indicative, the subjunctive and also the imperative and the conditional are 'moods'.

The present tense we have already revised is the *present indicative*. The indicative is used to express facts. The subjunctive puts an emphasis on the subject's feelings about the facts. It often implies a point of view. The link: subjunctive/subjective helps some people understand this. This may sound daunting but with practice it falls into place.

The uses you met here are:

1. The subjunctive after verbs of opinion, belief.

Tiziana wants to avoid sounding too categorical, she doesn't want to present what she says as fact. The subjunctive is used after verbs which convey this idea such as **credere, pensare,** etc. which introduce opinions, beliefs, etc.

2. The subjunctive after verbs expressing doubt.

Tiziana says:

Spero che la gente mi veda in questa maniera.
I hope people see me in this way.

Tiziana's subconscious choice to use **sperare** would indicate that she is unsure whether in fact that is the way people see her. In other words, she is expressing her doubts. Verbs of doubting are another group which require the subjunctive, e.g. **dubitare.**

Sperare is sometimes used without a subjunctive. The speaker is then not implying doubt.

Other verbs which are commonly followed by the subjunctive are verbs expressing fear (e.g. **ho paura che**) and desire (e.g. **desidero che**). Look at the list in the Grammar reference.

3. Note that Tiziana says:

Credo di avere un viso.
I think I have a face.

When the subject of both verbs is the same, a different structure is used, **di** + infinitive:

Credo che Tiziana sia molto attraente.
I think Tiziana is very attractive.

Credo di essere molto attraente.
I think I am very attractive.

Tiziana pensa che suo marito sia simpatico.
Tiziana thinks her husband is nice.

Tiziana pensa di essere simpatica.
Tiziana thinks she is nice.

Exercise 4

Tiziana is describing herself and her family. Change her statements as in the examples.

La mamma è molto magra.
Penso <u>che</u> la mamma <u>sia</u> molto magra.
Sono molto magra.
Penso <u>di essere</u> molto magra.

1 Mio padre è una persona disponibile.
2 Mia madre dà molta importanza alla famiglia.
3 I miei fratelli lavorano troppo.
4 Ho un atteggiamento positivo verso la vita.
5 I miei nonni sono affettuosi.
6 Sono una persona intraprendente.

Exercise 5

Here is a list of adjectives for describing character. You will know some of them and can probably guess at quite a few. Try the exercise below *before* reaching for the dictionary.

accomodante depresso noioso socievole affettuoso
egoista ottimista solare affidabile estroverso
parsimonioso solitario aggressivo flessibile pauroso
spendaccione allegro forte pessimista spiritoso
altruista freddo pigro stupido aperto inaffidabile
prepotente suscettibile attivo inflessibile presuntuoso
temerario avventuroso intelligente prudente
testardo cauto interessante rigido testone chiuso
introverso scorbutico triste coraggioso mite sereno
cordiale nervoso severo

A list of words like this is probably daunting. However, if you look more closely, there is much to help you guess meaning. An awareness of similarities between English and Italian suffixes can help, for instance.

1 What word ending(s) do you find that seem to be the equivalent of the English '-ous'? Does that help you guess any words?
2 What ending(s) seem to be the equivalent of the English '-able', '-ible'?
3 Your attention was earlier drawn to the use of the suffix -one, meaning 'big'. Does that help you guess any of these words?
4 What is the equivalent suffix to the English '-ist'?
5 If you do not know the words solare, spendaccione, what clues do they offer?

Exercise 6

Tiziana is describing her family again. She is saying what characteristics *she* thinks they have, and what *they* think they are like. As in every self-respecting family, they don't seem to agree! Look at the table below: in column A you will find what Tiziana thinks of the members of her family; in column B you will find what the members of her family think of themselves. Write a paragraph for each member of her family as if you were Tiziana.

Example: **Penso che mio padre sia un uomo molto testone. Lui, invece, pensa di essere una persona accomodante.**

	A	B
Her father	Stubborn	Adaptable
Her mother	Strict; very active, hard working	Flexible; rather lazy
Her brother	Quite attractive and sexy; a little bit too cautious	Quite ugly; fairly adventurous
Her sister	Extrovert, sociable; selfish	Shy but generous and loving

Ligabue © *La Stampa*

Text   Luciano Ligabue 🎧

Ligabue, a well-known singer, usually referred to by his surname only,
*calls himself 'il re del rock italiano'. He is a **cantautore**, that is he*
*writes his own material. The **cantautori** are an Italian tradition. Here*
are some extracts from an interview with him, in the same series as the
interview of Ricci.

Exercise 7

Do this exercise before listening to the recording.

This time we are involving you in the interview. Here are the interviewer's questions but not in order. And we give you Ligabue's
answers. Work out which question goes with which answer. Then
check your answers in the Key to exercises. The questions have been
numbered and the answers given letters. Use the grid below to record
your answers. Number one is done for you.

1 Sua moglie che tipo è?
2 Si considera un musicista?
3 Lei è un uomo e un marito fedele?
4 Che vita fa?
5 Il suo carattere?
6 Mettiamola così: si considera un uomo serio?

Answers	A	B	C	D	E	F
Questions	4					

DOMANDA   _____

LIGABUE   A cavallo tra le luci, i lustrini di un personaggio pubblico e la tranquillità di tornare a casa mia. A Correggio sto con gli amici, i miei affetti, leggo, scrivo, suono musica, vado al cinema e, se posso, produco nuovi musicisti. (A)

DOMANDA   _____

LIGABUE   Stiamo insieme da sette anni e siamo sufficientemente diversi per continuare a star bene insieme. (B)

DOMANDA   _____

LIGABUE   Inquieto con una grandissima smania di vivere, suscettibile e umorale. Passo da grandi entusiasmi a grandi down. (C)

DOMANDA   _____

LIGABUE   Sì, credo di sì. Sono un autore di canzoni e un cantante. (D)

DOMANDA   _____

LIGABUE   Questi sono un po' affari miei. (E)

DOMANDA   _____

LIGABUE   Mi considero una persona che ha grande rispetto per le persone che gli stanno vicino. (F)

Adapted from: *La Stampa*, 20 September 1998

Vocabulary ✦

a cavallo tra   lit. astride. Ligabue's life means his time is
divided between two very different worlds, the
public life of 'showbiz' and his private, home life.

lustrini   sequins

Correggio   Ligabue was born in Correggio, a small town
near Carpi, and his home is there. Carpi
(**da non confondere con Capri!**) is in
Emilia Romagna in the province of Modena.

grandi down   moments of depression (**down** is an English
word, Ligabue uses it as a noun. Using
English expressions (sometimes incorrectly)
is a characteristic of many areas of Italian life,
particularly the pop music and media scenes)

Language points ✦

Asking questions

Asking questions is easy in Italian: for questions expecting the answer
'yes' or 'no' you use tone of voice, with a rising intonation; or in
writing, just add a question mark:

Lei è un uomo e un marito fedele?
Are you a faithful man and husband?

Si considera un musicista?
Do you consider yourself a musician?

The interview questions used various *question words*. Here is a fuller
list (see Grammar reference):

Quando?	When?
Dove?	Where?
Come?	How?
Perché?	Why?
Quanto? Quanti?	How much? How many?
Chi?	Who?
Che cosa?	What? (often: **Cosa?** sometimes: **Che?**)
Quale? Quali?	Which? (**Qual?** in front of è, **era** – no apostrophe)

Exercise 8

You are spending a month in Italy in a small block of flats. You are curious about a family of neighbours, who seem to have peculiar habits. You seek information from the owner of the coffee bar down the street where you are staying. You want to know:

1 their names
2 where they are from
3 what language they speak
4 how long they have been living there
5 what job they do
6 how old they are
7 how many children they have
8 how old their children are
9 how many dogs they have
10 why they are always up all night
11 who rings them every night at 3
12 why they answer the phone and then start hoovering

Language learning suggestions

At the end of a unit before moving on, it pays dividends to remind yourself of what you have been learning. This is probably best done at the start of your next session. It is widely accepted that to revise something soon after you have learned it helps you to retain it. Look back to the objectives for the chapter listed at the beginning and see whether you feel you have achieved them. The first objective for this chapter related to describing people. Go back over the chapter listing the words and phrases which will help you to do this. Just listing them should prove a useful first step in learning them. Revising them from time to time and, more interestingly, using them will help fix them in your mind. And don't forget to work out. Try thinking out how to describe yourself and other people.

5 Ci siamo incontrati così

In this unit you will

▶ learn more about giving information about your personal history
▶ revise talking about the past, the perfect tense
▶ distinguish between transitive and intransitive verbs
▶ learn about agreement between pronouns and past participles
▶ meet **per** + expressions of time – saying how long you did/intend to do something before stopping

Dialogue 1

Sylvia asks the Coricas, Lalla and Angelo, how they met.

Exercise 1

1 Lalla and Angelo's romance began well but it also presented the young couple with a challenge. After reading the passage, try to explain this.
2 What attitudes does Lalla have which must have helped to make the marriage work?

SYLVIA	Come vi siete incontrati?
LALLA	Ma, nella maniera più romantica possibile: durante un valzer in un veglione di Carnevale.

SYLVIA	Ma Lei è proprio di qui, di Torino, vero?
LALLA	Io sono nata a Torino, figlia di torinesi, piemontesi da vecchia data.
SYLVIA	E invece Lei?
ANGELO	Io sono calabrese. Ero a Torino da pochi anni e per caso durante una festa di Carnevale, un veglione di Carnevale, in un grande salone, ho invitato Lalla a ballare con me il valzer e ci siamo conosciuti così.
SYLVIA	Ho capito.
ANGELO	Nell'anno 1958.
LALLA	Che era, devo aggiungere, molto difficile per l'integrazione Nord-Sud in Italia. Nel '58 . . . le persone che venivano dal Sud erano guardate con molto sospetto dalle persone che vivevano al Nord. Ecco, diciamo, non c'era ancora la Lega ma c'era questa fortissima resistenza razziale, e noi abbiamo deciso di passare sopra questi problemi razziali, insomma. A me son sempre piaciute molto le sfide, detesto i pregiudizi, credo che nella diversità ci sia veramente lo stimolo per qualcosa di buono, se riusciamo a tirarlo fuori. Non nascondo che è molto faticoso, ma . . . mi sembra che funzioni.

Vocabulary ♦

un veglione	a ball (formed from **veglia,** night, eve, vigil and **-one;** has come to mean a ball, often masked, lasting all night)
da vecchia data	for a long time (**da** = 'for' when the action/state is still going on – see Unit 1)
un fenomeno di antica data	an ancient phenomenon
un fenomeno di fresca data	a recent phenomenon Note: stress falls on **o**
Carnevale	The period, in February/March, according to the date of Easter, just before the start of Lent. Parties and balls, often masked, are traditional.
Torino	Italy's fourth largest city, capital of the Piedmont region, 'Turin' in English – and in the local dialect too.

ero a Torino da pochi anni	I had only been in Turin for a few years
salone	ballroom (a large room used usually for meetings, balls, special events, from **sala** 'reception room' (usually spacious) + **-one**)
ci siamo conosciuti così	that is how we met
ecco	Here the word has little meaning: 'so, well'. (Common in spoken Italian.)
la Lega	La Lega Nord, a political party which stands for regional autonomy and is opposed to centralised power exercised from Rome. (See Appendix 1.)
a me son sempre piaciute le sfide	I always liked challenges (**son** = **sono**. It is not unusual to drop the final vowel)
insomma	lit. in short, to sum up (often used in spoken Italian with less meaning, perhaps: 'so, there you are')
credo che nella diversità ci sia ... lo stimolo ...	Note the subjunctive after the expression of opinion.
mi sembra che funzioni	Another subjunctive after the expression of opinion.

Exercise 2

The passage below refers to the conversation above but there are blanks. Can you fill the blanks by adapting from the dialogue?

> Example: **Lalla e Angelo __ ____ _____ (incontrarsi) a un ballo di Carnevale.**
> **Lalla e Angelo <u>si sono</u> <u>incontrati</u> a un ballo di Carnevale.**

Lalla e Angelo si sono incontrati durante un veglione di Carnevale nel 1958. Angelo ____ _____ (1. invitare) Lalla a ballare con lui il valzer e __ ____ _____ (2. conoscersi) in questo modo. Naturalmente in seguito __ ____ _____ (3. innamorarsi) e ____ _____ (4. decidere) di sposarsi. Era un momento difficile in Italia: c'era una forte resistenza razziale nel Nord e le persone che vivevano al Nord guardavano con molto sospetto quelli che venivano dal Sud. Ma a Lalla ____ sempre _____ (5. piacere) le sfide.

In this exercise we asked you to use:

The perfect tense

The perfect or **passato prossimo** has two parts:

1 The present tense of **avere** or **essere**. This is known as the auxiliary verb.
2 The past participle of the verb you are using.

The past participle

The form of **the past participle** is similar but slightly different for each of the three types of regular verbs:

	Group 1: -**are** incontr**are**	Group 2: -**ere** conosc**ere**	Group 3: -**ire** cap**ire**
past participle	-**ato** incontr**ato**	-**uto** conosc**iuto**	-**ito** cap**ito**
perfect tense	ho incontr**ato**	ho conosc**iuto**	ho cap**ito**

Note: The **i** in **conosciuto**. It reminds us that the soft 'sh' sound is kept, so the spelling has to reflect this. -**scu** would be pronounced 'sk' (cf. **scusi**).

Exercise 3

Work out the past participles of the following verbs:

Example: **saltare – saltato**

> parlare sapere spedire trovare dovere uscire
> aspettare tenere dormire cantare volere finire

Use

The perfect is used to express a completed action in the past. Angelo said, for instance:

Ci siamo conosciuti così.
That is how we met.

Avere or *essere*? Which do you use?

1 Transitive verbs use avere (<u>ho</u> invitato Lalla a ballare). (For an explanation of 'transitive', see below.)

2 Intransitive verbs use either essere (<u>sono</u> nata a Torino) or avere. A great many of them take avere. It can be helpful to know that many of the verbs which use essere are verbs expressing movement: 'coming', 'going', 'arriving', 'leaving', 'going up and down', e.g. andare, venire, etc.; or verbs related to state or change of state and including: stare, essere, diventare.

3 All reflexive and reciprocal verbs use essere (<u>ci siamo incontrati a un ballo di Carnevale</u>).

When you use essere, the past participle has to agree in gender and number with the *subject*:

Maria è usci<u>ta</u> alle 8 (feminine singular)

Marco è usci<u>to</u> alle 8 (masculine singular)

Maria e Anna sono usci<u>te</u> alle 8 (feminine plural)

Marco e Francesco sono usci<u>ti</u> alle 8 (masculine plural)

For agreement of the past participle with verbs conjugated with avere see below.

Transitive and intransitive verbs

1 **Transitive verbs** are those which can have a direct object. An object is the person, or the thing, that receives the action of the verb (see Unit 3, Language points: More pronouns, b). A direct object answers the question 'what?' or 'who?' asked after the verb, e.g.:

John is writing a letter.   What is John writing?
A letter = direct object

John loves Mary.   Who does John love?
Mary = direct object

Sometimes the direct object is implied rather than expressed:

John is writing.

'To write' is still a transitive verb, although no direct object is expressed. There is a potential for a direct object.

A direct object can be a string of words:

Mary decided to marry John.   What did Mary decide?
To marry John = direct object

2 **Intransitive verbs** are those which cannot have a direct object. Very common intransitive verbs, which use **essere** to form the **passato prossimo**, are those which express motion (e.g. **andare**) and its opposite (e.g. **restare**), or change (e.g. **diventare**). Look at the list in the Grammar reference. However, as a great number of intransitive verbs take **avere**, when in doubt use **avere** rather than **essere**.

Exercise 4

Rewrite the sentences below in the perfect tense, thinking particularly about whether to use **essere** or **avere**. The first one is completed as an example.

1 La sera di Carnevale del 1958, Lalla <u>si prepara</u> per andare a un veglione.

   La sera di Carnevale del 1958, Lalla <u>si è preparata</u> per andare a un veglione.

2 **Si veste, si trucca, si pettina.**
3 **Chiama** un taxi.
4 Quando il taxi **arriva, sale** sul taxi e **dà** l'indirizzo al tassista.
5 Alla fine della corsa, **paga** il tassista ed **esce** dal taxi.
6 **Entra** nel salone della festa.
7 Angelo e Lalla **si incontrano** per caso, e Angelo **invita** Lalla a ballare.
8 Angelo e Lalla **ballano** un valzer.
9 Quando il valzer **finisce, cominciano** a chiacchierare.
10 Alla fine della serata, Angelo **domanda** a Lalla il suo numero di telefono.

Dialogue 2

Sandra asks Marco and Bea how they met.

Exercise 5

1 Why do you think Bea recalls the date of her meeting with Marco so clearly?
2 It could be said that their meeting was attributable to one of Bea's bad habits. What was it?
3 Was it love at first sight?
4 Where does the fact that they both play bridge fit into the story?

MARCO	Ci siamo incontrati all'università.
BEA	Ci siamo conosciuti il 30 ottobre dell'86, il giorno del mio ventesimo compleanno, e io come al solito ero arrivata in ritardo a scuola . . . era già stato occupato il mio posto dove mi sedevo di solito. Allora sono andata a sedermi in fondo, vicino a un mio amico, e gli ho detto di farmi gli auguri perché era il mio compleanno. Marco, che era seduto davanti a me, se ne è accorto e mi ha fatto gli auguri.
MARCO	Quando è finita l'ora, sì, ti ho fatto gli auguri.
BEA	Esattamente.
MARCO	E così ci siamo conosciuti. Poi siamo rimasti amici per tanto tempo, senza alcuna . . . alcun interesse. Poi . . . quanto tempo dopo? Non mi ricordo neanche . . .
BEA	Sette anni dopo . . . nel '93 . . . '94 . . .
MARCO	. . . giocando a bridge . . . abbiamo cominciato a frequentarci con una maggiore intensità . . . assiduità . . . e lì è scoccata . . .
BEA	. . . la scintilla . . .
MARCO	. . . chiamala scintilla! E allora poi, tre anni dopo, quattro anni dopo, nel '98, ci siamo sposati, il 25 aprile del '98.

Vocabulary ♦

scuola	Here Bea means 'class' in the university.
se ne è accorto	he noticed it (my friend wishing me Happy Birthday)
siamo rimasti amici per tanto tempo	we stayed friends (perhaps 'just friends) for a long time'
è scoccata la scintilla	the spark(s) flew (possibly we might say 'lightning struck')

Language points ♦

Again, Marco and Bea use the perfect tense as they recall meeting and the steps in their relationship, in some cases with identical verbs to the Coricas:

ci siamo incontrati
ci siamo conosciuti

Exercise 6

Can you pick out the remaining steps in Marco and Bea's relationship?

The perfect tense: form, part 2

- Some verbs have an irregular past participle. This is true of many verbs in the second group, -ere verbs. Above you had:

  accorgersi – accorto (this particular verb can only be used reflexively)

  rimanere – rimasto

There were also:

fare – fatto
dire – detto

The Grammar reference contains a list of common irregular past participles.

- Some verbs can use either **avere** or **essere** according to whether they are being used transitively or intransitively. Here are some examples to illustrate this:

  Paola <u>ha cambiato casa</u>: è andata ad abitare in un appartamento più grande.
  Paola <u>has moved house</u>. She has gone to live in a larger apartment.

  Marco <u>ha cambiato 500 euro</u> in dollari, perché domani parte per gli Stati Uniti.
  Mark <u>changed 500 euros</u> into dollars because he is leaving for the US tomorrow.

  Paola <u>è cambiata</u> molto: è dimagrita e ha fatto la permanente.
  Paola <u>has changed</u> a lot: she has lost weight and has had her hair permed.

  Il tempo <u>è cambiato</u> all'improvviso: fino a ieri ha fatto bello, e oggi fa di nuovo freddo.
  The weather <u>has</u> suddenly <u>changed</u>: it was lovely until yesterday, and today it's turned cold again.

- NB: Some verbs are transitive in English and intransitive in Italian, e.g. **telefonare a** – 'to ring'; **obbedire a** – 'to obey'; **assomigliare a** – 'to resemble'; **entrare in** – 'to enter'.

- Others are intransitive in English and transitive in Italian, e.g. **cercare** – 'to look for'; **aspettare** – 'to wait for'; **pagare** – 'to pay for'.

- With verbs conjugated with **avere**, the past participle agrees with a direct object pronoun, i.e. **lo, la, li, le.**

  La torta? L'abbiamo finit<u>a</u>.
  The cake? We've finished it.

  Li ho vist<u>i</u> stamattina.
  I saw them this morning.

With the pronouns **mi, ti, ci, vi,** if they are the direct object, there may be agreement but it is optional. If you intend to make this agreement, it is important to be aware of whether **mi, ti, ci, vi** are direct or indirect objects.

<u>Ti</u> ho salutat<u>a</u> / salutat<u>o</u>, ma tu non <u>mi</u> hai vist<u>a</u> / vist<u>o</u>. (direct)
I said hallo to you but you didn't see me.

<u>Ci</u> hanno aiutat<u>i</u> / aiutat<u>o</u> a fare il trasloco. (direct)
They helped us to move house.

<u>Vi</u> ho parlat<u>o</u> dell'Italia. (indirect)
I talked to you about Italy.

With **ne**, referring to a noun or pronoun, it is usual to make the agreement, but not when it refers to a phrase.

Quanti libri hai comprato? <u>Ne</u> ho comprat<u>i</u> dieci.
How many books did you buy? I bought ten.

Hai parlato con Paolo del fatto che non avrai ferie quest'estate? Sì, <u>ne</u> abbiamo parlat<u>o</u>.
Did you talk to Paolo about the fact that you won't have holidays this summer?
Yes, we talked about it.

This is quite a tricky area. It is one you should perhaps not worry about too much. We include the point for the sake of completeness and for the more advanced students.

Exercise 7

Read the sentences below and decide whether the verbs are used transitively. Underline the correct answer. When the verb is used transitively, underline the direct object (DO).

Example: crescere
Ho cresciuto <u>dieci figli</u> (DO).   transitive   intransitive
Sono cresciuto in Italia.   transitive   <u>intransitive</u>

1 correre   Ho corso la maratona.   transitive   intransitive
  Sono corso in suo aiuto.   transitive   intransitive
2 scendere   Sono sceso al piano di sotto.   transitive   intransitive
  Ho sceso le scale.   transitive   intransitive
3 migliorare   Ho migliorato il record del mondo.   transitive   intransitive
  La sua salute è migliorata.   transitive   intransitive
4 peggiorare   Ho peggiorato la situazione.   transitive   intransitive
  La mia salute è peggiorata.   transitive   intransitive
5 saltare   Sono saltato sul treno in corsa.   transitive   intransitive
  Ho saltato due giorni di scuola.   transitive   intransitive

6	finire	Ho finito di studiare alle otto di sera.	transitive	intransitive
		Il film è finito alle dieci.	transitive	intransitive
7	cominciare	Il film è cominciato alle sei.	transitive	intransitive
		Ho cominciato a lavorare nel 1998.	transitive	intransitive

Saying how long you did something. *Per* + expressions of time

In Unit 1, you revised the use of **da** with a present tense to express the idea of doing something for a period of time. This structure assumes the action is still being done.

Siamo amici da tanto tempo.
We have been friends for a long time.

This implies that they are still friends now.

To say you did something for a certain amount of time, with the implication that you no longer do it, that the action/state has ended, you use instead: **per.**

Siamo rimasti amici per tanto tempo.
We remained (just) friends for a long time.

But of course now they are more than friends, their friendship developed into a love which led to marriage.

Sono stato in Italia per 15 giorni.
I was in Italy for a fortnight (I am now back home).

Sono in Italia da 15 giorni.
I have been in Italy for a fortnight (I am still in Italy as I am speaking).

Exercise 8

Make pairs of sentences with the words in brackets and then say what each means.

Example: 1 **(studiare l'italiano – 10 anni)**

Ho studiato l'italiano per 10 anni.
I studied Italian for 10 years (I am not studying it any more).

Studio l'italiano da 10 anni.
I have been studying Italian for 10 years (I am still studying it).

2 (uscire con Francesca – 3 mesi)
3 (essere a dieta – 10 giorni)
4 (vivere in Canada – 40 anni)
5 (frequentare il corso di yoga – 5 settimane)
6 (cantare in un coro – 6 mesi)
7 (lavorare in banca – 15 anni)

Text

Exercise 9

Here are some Lonely Hearts advertisements from a national news-paper. Read them carefully and see whether you can suggest some possible pairings.

Annunci per Lui

Maria, 39enne bella, serena ed equilibrata, proprietaria di un noto ristorante, cerca uomo sensibile e generoso, amante della famiglia, per relazione importante.

Luisa, commerciante 39enne, bionda, sicura e decisa, cerca uomo max 55enne, amante dei viaggi e soprattutto degli animali, disposto a condividere la sua passione per gli animali e a rispettarla come merita.

Annunci per Lei

Francesco, dirigente vedovo 49enne senza figli, di bell'aspetto, elegante e curato, appassionato di cinema, cerca donna max 40enne amante viaggi per convivenza ed eventuale matrimonio.

Maurizio, commercialista 40enne, personalità brillante e decisa, amante cavalli, senza figli, cerca piacevole, intelligente compagna, max 46enne per costruire rapporto sentimentale.

Franca, 49enne commerciante vedova, solare e sportiva, amante del cinema, della lettura e delle passeggiate in montagna, cerca compagno max 60enne, indipendente e disponibile a lunghi viaggi.

Eleonora, 38enne, impiegata pubblica amministrazione, attiva e altruista, amante dell'arte, dei musei e del cinema, cerca compagno max 60enne per iniziare un serio rapporto sentimentale e per eventuale convivenza.

Aldo, ingegnere 40enne, alto, prestante, comunicativo, cerca signora amante della buona cucina e delle passeggiate, anche con figli, per legame affettuoso e possibile matrimonio.

Umberto, 57enne, dirigente, premuroso e ottimista, amante della musica lirica, della lettura e della montagna, cerca signora max 60enne, elegante, romantica, per vivere una vita serena.

Vocabulary ♦

31 enne, 39 enne	31-years-old, 39-years-old
max	Usual abbreviation for **massimo**.

Language learning suggestions

Use every opportunity which comes your way to try your Italian: in an Italian restaurant, greet the waiter in Italian. If he is not too busy he will enjoy your efforts. If you can, go to an Italian film, preferably with English subtitles. Perhaps you have an Italian neighbour or a colleague you can try the occasional conversation with. Buy an Italian magazine to look through. Try to get hold of some Italian music to sing along to . . . And don't forget about thinking in Italian when you have a spare moment.

6 Studi e carriera

In this unit you will

▶ practise talking about the past
▶ meet irregular past participles
▶ give information about your education and your experiences
▶ learn how to use Italian verbs followed by **di** and **a**
▶ meet the gerund

Dialogue 1

Listen to what Angelo Corica says about his early years as a doctor, then answer the questions.

Exercise 1

1 What sort of career did Angelo have in mind as a young man? And what did he eventually do?
2 Why did he leave Bologna?

ANGELO   Ho studiato medicina e mi sono laureato. Dopodiché ho fatto il militare, ufficiale medico, alla scuola per ufficiali medici a Firenze ... su in collina verso Piazzale Michelangelo ...

Poi ho iniziato un corso di specializzazione con la speranza di fare carriera universitaria a Bologna. Sulle prime un professore mi ha tenuto buono facendo delle promesse, dopodiché però, passato un anno, queste promesse non sono state mantenute, mio padre era morto, le mie finanze erano al verde ... molto al verde! Così nel '53 ho lasciato

Bologna e sono venuto a Torino. E qui ho iniziato la mia vita, con una certa difficoltà, si capisce. Ho fatto diverse sostituzioni nelle condotte piemontesi, mi sono un pochettino rinsanguato economicamente, e dopo varie vicissitudini, ho cominciato a fare quello che volevo fare, tutto sommato, fare il medico di famiglia.

Vocabulary ♦

mi sono laureato	I graduated, I got my degree
ho fatto il militare	I did my military service (**militare** = soldier). Military service has long been part of life for young Italian men. At the time of writing, it is being phased out.
Piazzale Michelangelo	A large square on the hill overlooking – and with a fine view of – Florence.
sulle prime	at first
mi ha tenuto buono	he kept me quiet, he kept me waiting
facendo delle promesse	by making promises (**facendo**: gerund)
dopodiché	then, next, after which
al verde	broke
si capisce	obviously, it goes without saying (lit. it is understood, one understands)
le condotte	**Una condotta** is a medical practice set up by a **comune**, a local authority.
mi sono rinsanguato economicamente	**Sangue** = 'blood', so Angelo got a financial blood transfusion, his financial situation improved.
tutto sommato	When all's said and done, everything considered. Another little phrase much used in conversation.

Language points ♦

Irregular past participles

Angelo says:

> **ho fatto il militare**
> I did my military service

> **ho fatto diverse sostituzioni**
> I did various locums

mio padre era morto
my father had died

Fatto, morto are the irregular past participles of **fare** and **morire**. A number of common verbs, especially in the second (-**ere**) group, have irregular past participles.

Exercise 2

Write down the past participles of the following verbs:

decidere   rispondere   mettere   essere   scrivere   vivere

One way of learning irregular past participles is to group them according to their form. We have done this – see the Grammar reference.

Exercise 3

In the bracketed phrases below you will find the outline of the life story of an engineer. Retell the story, using the perfect tense, as if it were yours. NB: All but four of the verbs have irregular past participles. Regular are: **studiare** (2), **laurearsi** (3), **lavorare** (7) and **andare** (9).

Examples: **(nascere a Bari – 1933)   Sono nato a Bari nel 1933.**
(**vivere a Bari – 19 anni) Ho vissuto a Bari per 19 anni.**

1 (iscriversi all'Università di Roma – 1952)
2 (studiare ingegneria – 5 anni)
3 (laurearsi in ingegneria civile – 1957)
4 (rimanere a Roma; lavorare per il Comune – 1 anno)
5 (fare il servizio militare in Sicilia)
6 (scegliere di vivere in una piccola città a nord di Roma, Grosseto; aprire uno studio privato con un collega – 1959)
7 (lavorare in proprio – 40 anni)
8 (scrivere per molte riviste specializzate, vincere alcuni appalti importanti)
9 (andare in pensione – 1999)
10 (essere in pensione – 3 anni)

With the help of Angelo's dialogue and your answers from the exercise, you should now be able to tell the story of your own career to date.

Dialogue 2))⑨

This is what Lalla Rossi, Angelo's wife, has to say about her early years. Listen and answer the questions.

Exercise 4

1 Why did Lalla not finish her degree?
2 What jobs does she mention enjoying particularly and why?
3 Once her children no longer needed her, what did she do?

LALLA   Io ho fatto gli studi superiori ma non ho terminato l'università e ho smesso di studiare perché terminate le scuole superiori era un periodo un po' di crisi per la mia famiglia, le mie sorelle hanno iniziato a lavorare, e ho iniziato a lavorare anch'io.

Poi ho tentato, lavorando, anche di studiare, ho dato alcuni esami, ho fatto alcuni anni di università, ma a dire la verità non ho avuto la perseveranza di arrivare alla fine, mi sono fermata a metà, ho preferito continuare a lavorare. Ho fatto dei lavori che mi sono piaciuti molto, mi è piaciuto molto il mondo del lavoro . . . mi è piaciuta l'indipendenza anche economica, mi è piaciuto viaggiare . . .

Un lavoro che mi è piaciuto molto è stato i due anni che ho fatto alla Comunità Europea a Bruxelles e . . . sono vissuta lì molto . . . come dire, da single, e mi è piaciuto tantissimo . . .

Tornando in Italia però quando ho avuto dei figli ho smesso di lavorare perché . . . perché volevo occuparmi della mia famiglia. Cosa che mi è piaciuta anche moltissimo e . . . ho trovato quello di occuparsi dei figli forse il lavoro più stimolante di tutti.

Tant'è vero che poi, quando le figlie sono state più grandi, sono entrata in un Consultorio Familiare, ho fatto un corso di preparazione, naturalmente, e questo è stato un lavoro di tipo volontario, ma molto importante nella mia vita, molto bello, che mi ha permesso di approfondire tante cose proprio sui legami famigliari, sull'educazione dei figli, sulla convivenza con il marito, coi parenti, eccetera.

Adesso basta, ho smesso tutto.

Vocabulary ♦

terminate le scuole superiori	when I had finished high school
ho tentato, lavorando, di studiare	I tried to study while working. Some faculties in Italian universities such as the humanities do not have an attendance requirement, so that this was a possible, but not an easy option. (Note: **lavorando** (gerund) = (here) while working)
ho dato alcuni esami	I sat some exams. Note: **dare un esame** = to sit an exam. Italian university courses work on a modular system, where you take a number of courses in a prescribed pattern, sitting an exam at the end of each one.
single	a person living alone. Much used in Italian nowadays.
ho smesso di lavorare	I stopped working. **Smesso** is the irregular past participle of **smettere**. cf. **mettere, messo**.
cosa che mi è piaciuta	something I enjoyed (lit. a thing which was pleasing to me)
ho trovato quello di occuparsi dei figli il lavoro più stimolante	I found looking after my children the most stimulating job
le figlie	Above Lalla referred to bringing up '**figli**', masculine, because she was referring to the task in a general sense. She herself had two daughters so here she uses the feminine form, thinking specifically of them.
consultorio familiare	(an advice centre for people with problems related to the family)
educazione (f)	upbringing (of children): a false friend. Education is: **istruzione** (f).
parenti (m.pl.)	relations. Another false friend: parents are: **i genitori**.
ho smesso tutto	I've stopped doing everything (Lalla has retired from her voluntary activities, from all commitments outside the family)

Language points ◆

Verbs followed by the infinitive: do they need *a* or *di* or nothing before the infinitive?

Lalla Rossi says:

ho smesso di studiare
I stopped studying, I gave up my studies

ho iniziato a lavorare
I started working

ho tentato di studiare
I tried to study

ho preferito continuare a lavorare
I preferred to continue working

mi è piaciuto viaggiare
I liked travelling

This is a tricky point. English is not a helpful point of reference: 'I tried to study' but 'I stopped studying'. Certain verbs in Italian can be followed by a second verb, in the infinitive. Some verbs require the preposition **a** before the second verb, others **di**. Some verbs require no preposition at all.

Most dictionaries tell you how a particular verb works. Any full list could be very long. We have put a selective list in the Grammar reference. Here are some useful verbs:

followed by **a**	followed by **di**	no preposition
cominciare a	finire di	volere
iniziare a	smettere di	potere
continuare a	decidere di	dovere
provare a	scegliere di	preferire
	cercare di	piacere

Note: In the perfect tense they all use the auxiliary **avere**. Exception: piacere
Also: Verbs with similar meaning (e.g. **cominciare/iniziare**) tend to work the same way, i.e. in this case, both need **a** before an infinitive.

Exercise 5

What did you do in . . .? Using the verbs listed below with the correct preposition **a, di,** or none, as appropriate, say what you began or tried to do or stopped doing, and in which year. Verbs marked (irr.) have an irregular past participle.)

Example: **Nel 1965 ho cominciato a studiare il giapponese.**

> cominciare continuare tentare potere smettere *(irr.)*
> finire cercare decidere *(irr.)* dovere volere provare
> scegliere *(irr.)* iniziare

Text 🔊

Italian society, along with that of other European countries, is changing, as people of other ethnic backgrounds are absorbed. This report which appeared in the national press in 1998 reflects this. The Arma dei Carabinieri is a proud institution. Here is the story of one rather unusual young recruit.

Exercise 6

Read the Text and answer the questions. You do not need to understand every word to get the gist:

1 Ange was one of three new trainees from non-Italian backgrounds. Can you say where the other two came from?
2 What is the relationship of Luciano Calloni and his wife to Ange?
3 Who did Ange meet when he went back to the Ivory Coast in 1992?
4 What did Ange find positive at the Cernaia Barracks during his training course?
5 Why do you think Ange was moved by the applause of the Nigerian prostitutes?

E' nato in Costa d'Avorio uno dei 500 nuovi allievi
'Io, carabiniere di colore'
Primo giuramento multietnico

'Quasi sono sbiancato per l'emozione'. Ange Caliste Calloni, 19 anni, il primo allievo carabiniere di colore in forza alla Caserma Cernaia, ha giurato fedeltà alla Repubblica Italiana ieri mattina insieme ai 500 compagni del 217° corso, suggellando così il primo giuramento multietnico dell'Arma dei Carabinieri: oltre ad Ange Caliste, che è nato a Teulaplè in Costa d'Avorio, c'erano infatti anche un giovane malese ed un ragazzo argentino . . .

Ange Caliste, che significa 'un bell'angelo', è stato adottato 13 anni fa da Luciano Calloni, un medico dentista milanese, e dalla moglie. Lo hanno incontrato in una missione nel cuore della Costa d'Avorio, a 400 chilometri dalla costa. Adesso papà Luciano non nasconde la commozione: 'Ho pianto a vedere mio figlio cantare l'Inno di Mameli, né più né meno di tanti altri papà'. Lui, Ange Caliste, è un ragazzo aperto, simpatico, sincero: 'Sono stato fortunato a venire in Italia, anche se non ho mai interrotto i rapporti con la mia famiglia naturale. Nel '92 sono anche tornato in Costa d'Avorio ed ho incontrato mia madre. Lei voleva restassi là, ma io sono tornato in Italia, la mia vera famiglia è qua'.

Da allievo carabiniere, ha conosciuto Torino, dove non era mai stato: 'Alla Cernaia si sta davvero bene. Qui ho trovato compagni simpatici e disponibili, ed anche gli ufficiali si sono subito mostrati pieni di umanità'. E la città fuori dalla caserma? 'L'ho vista poco, in questi primi venti giorni. La vedrò meglio nei prossimi due mesi. Comunque ho fatto incontri simpatici. Quando vado a Porta Susa, per prendere il treno, incontro spesso altri giovani di colore. Ho parlato con qualcuno di loro, tutti mi hanno sempre incoraggiato. La scorsa settimana alcune nigeriane, che stavano acquistando il biglietto, mi sono venute incontro e mi hanno applaudito. Ho pensato che era bellissimo che ci sentissimo così vicini, nonostante io fossi carabiniere e loro prostitute. Non dovrei dirlo, ma mi sono commosso'.

Angelo Conti

Adapted from *La Stampa*, Sunday 21 June 1998

Vocabulary ♦

sono sbiancato	**sbiancare** = to turn white. The word can be used literally, referring for instance to bleaching linen, or to mean 'turn pale' from emotion. Ange is having a bit of fun with his words.
Caserma Cernaia	The barracks in Turin where new recruits are trained.
suggellando	sealing (gerund).
giuramento	**giurare** = to swear. The new trainees swear allegiance to the Italian Republic. The words which begin the oath are taken up in the title, 'I, black carabiniere'. It is usual to say 'di colore' in Italian, rather than 'nero' ('black').
multietnico	multiracial
medico dentista	dentist (Italian dentists do a medical training before specialising)
disponibili	willing to help (lit. available)
commozione	emotion. The verb is: **commuovere/commuoversi**, past participle: **commosso** moved, used by Ange later.
Porta Susa	One of the Turin railway stations, near the Cernaia barracks. Trains for Milan stop there.

Language points ♦

The gerund

The gerund has appeared three times in this unit as well as in earlier units.

* In the Text:

  suggellando così il primo giuramento multietnico
  in this way sealing the first multiracial oath of loyalty

* In what Angelo said:

  un professore mi ha tenuto buono facendo delle promesse
  a professor kept me quiet by making promises

* And in what Lalla said:

  ho tentato, lavorando, anche di studiare
  I tried, while working (at the same time), to study too

Form

The gerund is simple to form. Remove the infinitive ending of the verb and add -**ando** for Group 1 verbs and -**endo** for all others:

parl**are**	dare	stare	decid**ere**	cap**ire**	part**ire**	essere	avere
parlando	dando	stando	decidendo	capendo	partendo	essendo	avendo

Very few verbs are irregular. They are verbs with an infinitive which is a contracted form of an earlier infinitive, and their compounds:

bere	dire	fare	-durre *verbs, as* produrre	porre
< bevere	< dicere	< facere	< producere	< ponere
bevendo	dicendo	facendo	producendo	ponendo

Uses of the gerund

The gerund translates the idea: by, on, in, while doing something.

un professore mi ha tenuto buono facendo delle promesse
a professor kept me quiet by making promises

ho tentato, lavorando, anche di studiare
I tried while working, to study too

The subject of the main verb is automatically the subject of the gerund, i.e. both actions must be done by the same person. You need to be quite clear about what you mean. Compare:

Ho visto Paola attraversando la strada.
I saw Paola while (I was) crossing the street.

Ho visto Paola che attraversava la strada.
I saw Paola crossing the street. (Paola was crossing the street, not I.)

In the Text the sentence doesn't have a finite verb and Ange is still the subject:

suggellando così il primo giuramento multietnico
in this way sealing the first multiracial oath of loyalty

The gerund with an object or reflexive pronoun

Object and reflexive pronouns are attached to the end of the gerund and do not precede it. Angelo might have talked about the professor keeping him quiet:

facendomi delle promesse
by making me promises

Alzandosi dal letto, Giovanni è scivolato e si è rotto la gamba.
While getting out of bed, Giovanni slipped and broke his leg.

This is also true with other non-finite parts of the verbs (the infinitive, the past participle), hence the infinitives of reflexive verbs: alzarsi, divertirsi etc. (See Unit 2.)

Vorresti darmi il tuo numero di telefono e indirizzo email?
Would you give me your telephone number and email address?

The gerund is also used with the verb **stare** to form a continuous tense, when the intention is to underline the continuous nature of the action. We shall look at this more closely in Unit 9.

Exercise 7

You have now heard various life histories. Here are lists of the words used to tell them. Use them to tell your story:

vita personale, famiglia
nascere   morire   vivere   incontrarsi   conoscersi   frequentarsi
sposarsi, convivere   separarsi, divorziare   vivere da solo/a   essere sposato/a,
separato/a, divorziato/a, single   avere dei figli   occuparsi (dei figli, della
famiglia)   crescere / educare i figli   trasferirsi   lasciare (una città, il marito,
la moglie)

studi
diplomarsi   iscriversi a / studiare (Lettere, Medicina, Ingegneria, Economia,
Lingue, Giurisprudenza)   dare / passare un esame   laurearsi in
(Medicina)   terminare gli studi   seguire un corso di preparazione /
formazione / specializzazione

lavoro
fare pratica come (cuoco, avvocato)   fare il militare, il medico, il cuoco
trovare lavoro / lavorare come (cameriere, medico, cuoco)   fare carriera
fare un lavoro impegnativo, noioso   fare un lavoro volontario
lavorare nel volontariato

espressioni utili

per caso   però   così   ecco   esattamente   si capisce   naturalmente
diciamo   tutto sommato   a dire la verità   tant'è vero che   poi   allora
x anni dopo   dopodichè   eccetera (ecc.)

Language learning suggestion

Are you managing to set aside time for your Italian? Little and often is generally the best formula. It is difficult in a busy life, but how about your coffee break in the morning; or your lunch-time sandwich? Have your Italian book with you so that spare moments can be used. And when you are engaged in some manual activity such as cooking, driving somewhere, gardening, waiting for a bus or a train, something which doesn't require your full concentration, try thinking in Italian – about anything: what you are doing, a topic of current interest – it doesn't matter what, but give yourself some practice – a workout.

7 Lavorare in Italia

In this unit you will

▶ learn about some of the findings of the 2001 Census
▶ learn the procedures involved in taking foreign staff onto the payroll of an organisation in Italy
▶ say you want to, have to and can do something: the modal verbs (**volere, dovere, potere**) – in the present, conditional and perfect tenses
▶ meet object pronouns with modal verbs

Text   Italy today

Immigration, mostly from Eastern Europe and Africa, has increased hugely in recent years. Many immigrants come in illegally. Italy has high unemployment and for this reason there are quotas, region by region, for non-European Union immigrants. The EU of course guarantees its nationals freedom of movement within the EU. Here is a newspaper article, reporting findings of the 2001 Census, as regards immigration.

E' **triplicato** il numero degli stranieri residenti nel nostro Paese: dieci anni fa erano **356.159**. Altri **252.185** non sono residenti

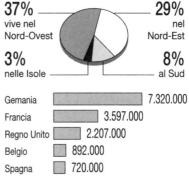

37%
vive nel
Nord-Ovest

29%
nel
Nord-Est

3%
nelle Isole

8%
al Sud

Gemania	7.320.000
Francia	3.597.000
Regno Unito	2.207.000
Belgio	892.000
Spagna	720.000

Adapted from: *Il Corriere della Sera*, 28 March 2000

Italia multirazziale

Gli stranieri sono tre volte di più

I dati del Censimento: cresce l'immigrazione, ogni mille italiani ci sono 17 extracomunitari.

Ogni mille italiani ci sono 17,5 stranieri, che salgono a 25 nel nord-ovest e a 27 nel nord-est: il triplo di dieci anni fa. In totale sono un milione e mezzo e sono in maggioranza giovani (il 19 % ha meno di 18 anni).

Gli stranieri sono ancora pochi in Italia a confronto con altri Paesi dell'Unione Europea, dove la presenza media è superiore a 50 unità ogni mille abitanti, praticamente il triplo e a volte il quadruplo rispetto all'Italia. In Germania sono il 9 % della popolazione, da noi meno del 2 %.

E comunque è chiaro: l'Italia è sempre più multiculturale, che piaccia o meno. Gli italiani-italiani, invece, sono in fase decrescente all'incirca dal 1981, e se il numero complessivo dei residenti resta lo stesso (56 milioni) lo si deve proprio all'incremento dell'immigrazione.

Raffaello Masci

Adapted from *La Stampa*, Thursday 28 March 2002

Exercise 1

Read the article and say whether the following statements are true or false:

1 17.5 per cent of the population of Italy are from outside the European Union.

2 The percentage of immigrants in the population is highest in the North-East.

3 The number of foreigners living in Italy has doubled in the last ten years.

4 Most immigrants are young.
5 For the European Union as a whole the average percentage of immigrants in the population is 5 per cent.
6 The decline in the number of native-born Italians in Italy began around 1981.
7 The population of Italy has increased since the last census.

Vocabulary ◆

stranieri	foreigners. The word is being used loosely to mean 'non EU citizens'.
extracomunitari	nationals of states which are not members of the European Union, formerly Community
a confronto con	compared with
unità	units (here actually one unit means one person)
rispetto a	compared with
che piaccia o meno	whether you like it or not
lo si deve a	it is due to

Dialogue 1

Maria Recrosio is Business Manager in an international school in northern Italy. The school has an American legal status and ethos. The teaching is in English. The school therefore recruits English-speaking teachers. Sylvia asks Maria about the procedure for taking on non-Italian staff who have been recruited by the Head Teacher. NB: The regulations/laws in this field are subject to change.

Exercise 2

Pick out the stages of the process to be gone through before the recruit is formally taken onto the payroll of the school. In the Key to exercises you will find not only the answer but some clarification of the procedure.

SYLVIA Che procedura deve seguire uno straniero che ha la cittadinanza di un altro Paese dell'Unione Europea e che viene a lavorare nella scuola?

MARIA Deve venire prima in Italia e chiedere il permesso di soggiorno. Quindi viene in anticipo, almeno un paio di mesi

	prima, va in Questura e chiede il permesso di soggiorno per lavoro.
SYLVIA	E può ottenere il permesso di soggiorno senza avere un lavoro preciso?
MARIA	No, normalmente facciamo una specie di contrattino in precedenza in cui si dice che questa persona verrà a lavorare da noi.
SYLVIA	Uno potrebbe chiedere il permesso di soggiorno anche senza avere un lavoro?
MARIA	Eh ... diventa più difficile. Si può fare anche. Però normalmente la procedura quando noi assumiamo qualcuno è come ti ho detto.
SYLVIA	E poi?
MARIA	Tornano nel Paese di provenienza e finiscono il loro lavoro. Poi ritornano da noi e a quel punto rimangono qui per almeno 20/25 giorni per ritirare il permesso di soggiorno e chiedere la residenza. Una volta che hanno il certificato di residenza possono chiedere il libretto di lavoro. Dopodiché, possiamo fare l'assunzione.
SYLVIA	Come per un italiano ...
MARIA	Come per un italiano, come per un italiano.

Vocabulary ♦

in anticipo	early
Questura	Police Headquarters. There is one for each province, so the employee needs to go to the main town of the province.
assumere	to engage (staff), put them on the payroll. Past participle: **assunto**; noun: **assunzione** (f).
paese di provenienza	the country they come from
si può fare	lit. one can do (it), i.e. it can be done.

Useful words and phrases

un colloquio	an interview
un datore di lavoro	an employer
un ufficio di collocamento	a job centre (publicly run centre for putting job seekers and potential employers in touch)

chiedere un permesso	
... **di soggiorno**	to ask for a permit to stay
... **di lavoro**	a work permit
... **per costruire**	permission to build
ritirare un documento	to collect a document (from the issuing authority)
un contratto di lavoro	a contract for a job
un libretto di lavoro	document which records details about the worker and his / her previous positions. **Libretto** is formed from **libro** + **-etto** = little.
un libretto sanitario	document which records entitlement to medical treatment with the Italian National Health Service (**Servizio Sanitario Nazionale**).
libretto di circolazione	car logbook, which records the details of the car and its ownership.
la patente di guida	driving licence
il codice fiscale	A combination of numbers and letters given to each taxpayer which identifies him/her in the files of the taxation authorities (National Insurance number in the UK).
la carta d'identità	identity card. All Italian citizens have one. Everyone in Italy must carry an identity document with them at all times. Nationals of other states resident in Italy may also apply for an Italian identity card which is more convenient to carry than a passport.
la partita IVA	For those who are liable to charge Value Added Tax (**Imposta sul Valore Aggiunto**) for their services, i.e. businesses or independent professionals, a number given by the tax authorities to such people or organisations.
il fisco	the tax authorities
fiscale	to do with tax, fiscal. Used colloquially to mean: petty-minded, hair-splitting, excessively precise; similar, less colloquial, is **pignolo**.

Language points ♦

Saying you 'want to', 'are able to' and 'have to' do something – the modal verbs: **volere, dovere, potere.**

All three verbs work the same way. They are followed by an infinitive *without* a preposition, i.e. you do not put in a word for 'to'.

(La persona) deve venire in Italia.
(The person) has to come to Italy.

Deve chiedere il permesso di soggiorno.
He/she has to ask for a permit to stay.

Può ottenere il permesso.
He/she can get a permit.

Voglio lavorare in Italia.
I want to work in Italy.

Object pronouns with *dovere, potere, volere*

In Unit 6, dealing with the gerund, you learned that object pronouns are placed after the gerund and written attached to it, and that this is also the case with the infinitive and with participles. When an object pronoun is used with **dovere, potere** or **volere** it can be placed either before **dovere, potere** or **volere** or attached to the accompanying infinitive:

Le tue foto sono qui. Le posso guardare? / Posso guardarle?
Your photos are here. May I look at them?

Il mio passaporto è scaduto: lo devo rinnovare. /
devo rinnovarlo.
My passport has expired: I must renew it.

All three verbs are irregular. **Dovere** has alternative forms in the present tense (1st person singular and 3rd person plural). The first form is more common.

Present tense

	volere	potere	dovere
1st sing	voglio	posso	devo/debbo
2nd sing	vuoi	puoi	devi
3rd sing	vuole	può	deve
1st plur	vogliamo	possiamo	dobbiamo
2nd plur	volete	potete	dovete
3rd plur	vogliono	possono	devono/debbono

Exercise 3

You live in Scotland and have asked an Italian friend for information about the procedures to follow for working in Italy. Your friend's answer has been printed with blanks. Each needs a part of either **dovere, potere** or **volere** and the infinitive of one of the verbs below. They are not listed in the correct order. You can use a verb more than once. Complete the letter. The first blank has been completed to show you what to do.

---

firmare aspettare richiedere cominciare venire ottenere andare lasciare mandare trovare fare dare cercare impiegare spedire

---

Cara Mary,

Se _vuoi trovare_ lavoro in Italia, 1_____ gli annunci di lavoro sul sito Internet www.cliccalavoro.it. Quando hai trovato il lavoro che ti interessa, 2_____ la tua domanda al datore di lavoro, 3_____ la risposta e 4_____ in Italia per il colloquio.

Se ti offrono il lavoro, ti 5_____ una dichiarazione scritta della promessa di lavoro. Con questa dichiarazione, 6_____ alla Questura, e 7_____ un Permesso di Soggiorno per Lavoro. Il tuo nuovo datore di lavoro 8_____ la richiesta per te.

Una volta che hai ottenuto il Permesso di Soggiorno, 9_____ il tuo lavoro in Scozia e venire di nuovo in Italia. In Italia, tu e il tuo datore di lavoro 10_____ in Comune con il Permesso di Soggiorno e 11_____ il Certificato di Residenza.

Con questo certificato, il tuo datore di lavoro 12_____ un libretto di lavoro dall'Ufficio di Collocamento e tu 13_____ il contratto di lavoro vero e proprio.

I tempi degli uffici in Italia sono molto lunghi, e 14_____ qualche mese per rilasciare il permesso di Soggiorno. Quindi, se sei interessata a lavorare in Italia l'anno prossimo, 15_____ a muoverti con buon anticipo!

Fammi sapere se ti 16_____ informazioni più dettagliate. Buona fortuna!

Marcello

Language points ♦

The three verbs **volere, potere, dovere** can be used in other tenses followed by an infinitive.

The conditional

One of the most useful tenses appears in the dialogue:

> Uno <u>potrebbe</u> chiedere il permesso di soggiorno senza avere un lavoro?
> <u>Could</u> one ask for a permit to stay without having a job?

This is the conditional of **potere**. For each of the three verbs the conditional is:

	endings	volere	potere	dovere
1st sing	-ei	vorrei	potrei	dovrei
2nd sing	-esti	vorresti	potresti	dovresti
3rd sing	-ebbe	vorrebbe	potrebbe	dovrebbe
1st plur	-emmo	vorremmo	potremmo	dovremmo
2nd plur	-este	vorreste	potreste	dovreste
3rd plur	-ebbero	vorrebbero	potrebbero	dovrebbero

(For a full treatment of the conditional, see Unit 8. See also the Grammar reference.)

Use

The conditional tense is used when a condition is expressed, or as in the example above, implied: i.e. 'If one wanted to, could one ask for a permit to stay without having a job?'

The three verbs are tricky in English in this tense and you need to think carefully about the meaning of the English:

1 **vorrei**: 'I should / would like', 'I'd like'. In addition, just as in English 'I'd like' sounds less imperious than 'I want', so **vorrei** is more courteous than **voglio**. Beware the English use of 'would' to mean 'used to' (e.g. 'when I lived in New York I would eat out most evenings') and where no condition is present or implied.
2 **potrei**: 'I could', 'I should/would be able to'.

3   **dovrei**: 'I should', 'I ought to' (NB: 'should' in English can mean 'ought', but is also used to form the conditional tense).

Vorrei ottenere un lavoro in Italia; potrei fare l'interprete o il traduttore.
I'd like to get work in Italy; I could be an interpreter or a translator.

E' tardi, dovremmo tornare a casa.
It's late, we ought to go home.

Exercise 4

Compromessi

Work dominates your life and you never have time for your own personal interests. You are trying to work out a better balance. Write down what you propose to do each day this week with the potential problems.

Example: **Lunedì sera: cinema – a letto presto – spettacolo delle 6**

Lunedì sera <u>vorrei andare</u> al cinema perché fanno gli sconti, ma <u>dovrei</u> anche <u>andare</u> a letto presto perché martedì sarà una giornata molto pesante al lavoro. Forse <u>potrei andare</u> allo spettacolo delle 6, invece che a quello delle 8,30.

1   martedì pomeriggio: piscina – riunione settimanale con il direttore – piscina all'ora di pranzo
2   mercoledì mattina: un po' di spesa – in ufficio dalle 9 alle 5 – dalle 10 alle 6
3   giovedì pomeriggio: i compiti per il corso di italiano – un appuntamento di lavoro a Milano – fare i compiti durante il viaggio in treno
4   Venerdì pomeriggio: fine settimana in montagua – appuntamento con un cliente importante – appuntamento con il cliente alla mattina

Language points ♦

The perfect tense of *volere, potere, dovere*

All three verbs have regular past participles:

volere	potere	dovere
voluto	potuto	dovuto

However, the choice of auxiliary depends on the infinitive which is to follow. If it is the infinitive of a verb conjugated with **esscre**, then when a modal verb precedes it, the modal verb is conjugated with **essere**.

<u>Sono voluto/a andare</u> all'università perché mi piace studiare.
I decided to go to college because I like studying.*

<u>Sono dovuto/a andare</u> in Questura.
I had to go to the Police Station.

Antonio non <u>è potuto venire</u> oggi.
Antonio could not come today.

With verbs conjugated with **avere**, **avere** is the auxiliary used.

Non <u>ho voluto fare</u> l'università perché non garantisce un buon lavoro.
I decided not to go to college because it is no guarantee of a good job.*

<u>Ho dovuto richiedere</u> il Permesso di Lavoro.
I had to request a Working Permit.

Non <u>ho potuto fare</u> la domanda.
I wasn't able to ask the question.

This is a difficult point and we recommend the learner not to worry too much about getting this right. If in doubt, use **avere**. It will not obscure your meaning.

*Note: we have translated **volere** by 'decide'. When **volere** is used in the perfect, an action is involved, it is a decision, a desire acted upon, rather than just a desire.

Exercise 5

You never manage to do what you ought to do and you always have to make excuses. Make some, on the lines of the example:

andare al supermercato – passare in tintoria

Mi dispiace! Non <u>sono potuto/a andare</u> al supermercato perché <u>sono dovuto/a passare</u> in tintoria.

1 prenotare la vacanza al mare – andare dal parrucchiere
2 depositare l'assegno in banca – lavorare fino a tardi

3 fare i compiti di italiano – accompagnare mia figlia a una festa
4 fare la spesa – andare dal dentista

Dialogue 2

In recent years in spite of it being American, the school where Maria works has tended to take more European Union nationals than Americans.

Exercise 6

1 The school would like to employ American teachers. Why has this American school employed European Union nationals rather than Americans recently?
2 Which category of employees finds it easier than other non-EU nationals to get a work visa?

MARIA   Il problema invece è per gli extracomunitari perché . . . noi dobbiamo chiedere l'autorizzazione di assumere un extracomunitario, che può essere un insegnante americano, quello che a noi può interessare. Solo che ultimamente hanno messo delle percentuali di ingresso per gli extracomunitari, quindi noi, non avendo la certezza di poter assumere extracomunitari, in questi ultimi due anni abbiamo preferito prendere solo cittadini comunitari. Perché, se poi l'autorizzazione viene negata perché la Regione ha già . . . raggiunto il numero di ingresso degli extracomunitari, dobbiamo poi cercare un altro candidato. E . . . la persona non è sicura di essere assunta. Questa incertezza non va né per la persona né per la scuola.

SYLVIA   Ma se l'autorizzazione c'è, di assumere un extracomunitario, poi la procedura . . .

MARIA   Noi dobbiamo mandare questo permesso per esempio negli Stati Uniti, dove devono andare al Consolato Italiano, farsi mettere un timbro sul passaporto, poi vengono in Italia, vanno in Questura, chiedono il permesso di soggiorno come per i cittadini dell'Unione Europea. Comunque la procedura poi è

> *semplice. La cosa più lunga è avere questa autorizzazione all'assunzione . . . ci vuol sempre del tempo . . .*
>
> SYLVIA   *E dipende dal lavoro che farà la persona?*
>
> MARIA   *C'è differenza tra un dirigente e il resto . . . diciamo delle assunzioni. Per ora diciamo sono agevolati i dirigenti.*

Vocabulary ◆

hanno messo delle percentuali	they've introduced percentages. 'They' being the government. Rather than 'percentages', in English one might say 'quotas'.
questa incertezza non va né per la persona né per la scuola	this uncertainty is no good, either for the person or for the school
la Regione	the region. Administratively Italy is divided into twenty regions. Each region is subdivided into provinces.
farsi mettere un timbro sul passaporto	have a stamp put on his/her passport (a visa stamp)
un timbro	rubber stamp
un francobollo	a postage stamp
sono agevolati i dirigenti	managers are given preference (lit. things are made easy for managers)
diciamo	lit. let's say. Another little 'prop' to use while you search for the right word, which is what Maria is doing here.

Useful phrases with *volere, potere, dovere*

Volere

volere (voler) dire	to mean
Che cosa vuol(e) dire 'extracomunitario'?	What does 'extracomunitario' mean?
volere (voler) bene a qualcuno	to be fond of someone

Volendo (gerund) is often used as a short way of saying:
if you want, if we want . . .

Volendo, possiamo anche rivedere il presente indicativo.	If you want, if we want, we can also revise the present indicative.
Volendo, possiamo organizzare un incontro.	If you want, we can organise a meeting.

Potere

Può darsi.	Maybe.
Può essere.	It may be the case.
Può andare.	It will do.
Non ne posso più.	I can't take any more, I can't go on, I am exhausted.

Dovere

Dev'essere vero.	It must be true.
Dev'essere pronto.	It must be ready.

Language learning suggestion

When you are thinking in Italian, forget sometimes that you are an adult and have sophisticated thoughts. Try instead to be a child again, think simple ideas, say them in simple ways. Learning another language is in some ways like becoming a child again. It also means to some extent taking on another personality – and that can be fun! Accept the limitations of your Italian but enjoy the new experience too!

8 Un colloquio di lavoro

In this unit you will

- consider more suffixes
- eavesdrop on a job interview
- meet the conditional of verbs other than **dovere, potere, volere**, etc.
- revise the imperative
- meet a further use of the subjunctive – in a specific type of adjectival clause
- consider how to guess meaning and use a dictionary

Text

Exercise 1

Look at this job advertisement and say whether the following statements are true or false.

1 Toys Center supplies specialists working with small children as well as the general public.
2 Toys Center has shops throughout Italy.
3 Toys Center needs a manager for their shop in Milan.
4 Candidates for the job must be over 35.
5 A degree is essential.
6 Candidates must have at least three years' experience in a position of responsibility.
7 It doesn't matter if they have never led a group or a team.
8 They must have computer skills.

TOYS center

Azienda leader nella vendita del giocattolo, giochi elettronici, articoli per la prima infanzia e puericultura, con oltre 60 filiali distribuite sul territorio nazionale, ricerca per prossima apertura a TORINO:

Responsabile di negozio

cui affidare l'organizzazione e la gestione economico-commerciale del punto vendita

Richiediamo:

* età non superiore ai 35 anni
* diploma di scuola media superiore
* esperienza almeno triennale in posizione di responsabilità (capo reparto, capo gruppo) maturata preferibilmente in aziende della G.D.O.
* spirito di iniziativa e sensibilità commerciale
* spiccata attitudine ai rapporti interpersonali e capacità di gestione di un gruppo di collaboratori
* l'abitudine all'uso dei principali strumenti informatici.

Offriamo:

inserimento in una società in forte sviluppo, attenta al riconoscimento del merito individuale.

Invitiamo gli/le interessati/e a inviare un curriculum corredato da foto, recapito telefonico ed autorizzazione al trattamento dei dati personali (ai sensi della legge 675/96 sulla privacy) a:

HOLDING DEI GIOCHI SPA – Direzione del Personale – Via Vitruvio 43 – 20124 MILANO

Vocabulary ♦

puericultura	lit. child-rearing. The study of the character, growth and development of children.
filiali	branches (sing: **filiale**, f)
triennale	(1) lasting three years (2) recurring every three years. In this case (1).
GDO	**Grande Distribuzione Organizzata** i.e. the big supermarket chains
distribuzione	retailing
sensibilità	sensitivity (a false friend!)
spiccata	marked, outstanding (m: **spiccato**)
corredato	**corredare** to provide everything necessary, here simply: with.
legge 675/96	Law no. 675 of 1996, which restricts use of personal data. Another law often mentioned in job advertisements is L.903/77 relating to equal opportunities for men and women.

Language points ♦

Suffixes

In Unit 3 we mentioned a second type of suffix which turns one class of word into another, for instance from verb into noun. The suffix -tore (m) / -trice (f) is a common one, indicating a person carrying out the action described by the corresponding verb; as are -zione / -sione / -ione (f – always) for the related noun.

coordinare – coordina<u>tore</u>/coordina<u>trice</u> – coordina<u>zione</u>
to coordinate – coordinator – coordination

The link: infinitive – past participle – adjective is common:

abituare – abitu<u>ato</u>
to accustom – accustomed, used to

conoscere – conosci<u>uto</u>
to know – known

Thinking 'links' is useful in guessing:

autorizzare – autorizza<u>zione</u> – autorizz<u>ato</u> – autorizza<u>tore</u>
to authorise – authorisation – authorised – authoriser

inserire – inser**imento** – inser**ito**
to insert – insertion – inserted

Exercise 2

Identify the suffix and translate the words:

(a) From the verb to the noun:

Example: **sciare – sciatore:** (scia**tore**) to ski – skier

1 conoscere – conoscitore:
2 vendere – venditrice:
3 gestire – gestore:
4 scrivere – scrittore:
5 leggere – lettrice:

(b) From the verb to the abstract noun:

Example: **sapere – sapienza** (sapi**enza**): to know – knowledge

1 conoscere – conoscenza:
2 provenire – provenienza:
3 gestire – gestione:
4 maturare – maturazione:
5 vendere – vendita:
6 crescere – crescita:

(c) Try to guess the meaning of these words and define them in Italian. Use words in the same 'family' to help you. Then check in a dictionary.

Example: **informatore (informare, informazione)**

your guess: una persona che informa
your (English) dictionary: an informant

1 ristoratore (ristorare, ristorazione, ristorante)
2 assicuratore (assicurare, assicurazione)
3 imbottigliatore (imbottigliare, imbottigliamento)

Dialogue 1

Elisa Cantoni, an interpreter / translator, is looking for work in Italy. Here she is being interviewed by a Milan fashion house.

Elisa

Exercise 3

1 Describe Elisa's work in England.
2 Why does she find this work satisfying?
3 Why does she want to change her job?

D.P. = Direttore del Personale

D.P.	Per cominciare, vorrei farLe alcune domande riguardo alla sua esperienza di lavoro. Ci spieghi le mansioni che svolge nel suo lavoro in Inghilterra.
ELISA	Volentieri. Prima di tutto collaboro all'organizzazione di sfilate londinesi stagionali per i designer Krizia e Missoni. Sono anche interprete per la sede londinese del Centro Fiorentino Pitti, che vende i suoi modelli a negozi d'alta moda britannici. Poi ... beh, c'è il mio lavoro come traduttrice, principalmente per Vogue Magazine On-Line. Curo l'edizione italiana on-line di questo giornale di moda.
D.P.	Come giudicherebbe la sua esperienza di lavoro all'estero?
ELISA	Entusiasmante, naturalmente, e piena di opportunità, direi. Fare da interprete a stilisti italiani all'estero mi ha portato a conoscere meglio il mondo internazionale della moda e sono sempre molto contenta ed orgogliosa di aiutare a diffondere in altri Paesi la creatività e l'eleganza delle collezioni italiane.
D.P.	Ci dica perché ha deciso di cambiare lavoro e di cercare lavoro in Italia.
ELISA	La mia intenzione sarebbe tornare a risiedere a Milano. Mi sono appena sposata e sia io che mio marito preferiremmo abitare in Italia. Dopo il trasferimento a

Milano, sarei comunque disponibilissima a viaggiare per lavoro. Vorrei però abbandonare il mio lavoro per le sfilate. Anche se lo adoro, mi lascia veramente poco tempo per la mia vita privata.

Vocabulary ♦

le mansioni	duties (in a job). Usually **svolgere mansioni,** to undertake duties.
beh	Well (what you say as you hesitate)
aiutare a	Note: **aiutare a +** infinitive.
ho deciso di	Note: **decidere di** + infinitive.
disponibilissima	very willing
disponibile	available. Note: **disponibile a fare qualcosa.**

Language points ♦

1. The conditional

You met the conditional of **volere, potere** and **dovere** in the previous unit. In this dialogue you hear other verbs in the conditional:

come <u>giudicherebbe</u>
how <u>would you judge</u>

<u>direi</u>
I'd say

la mia intenzione <u>sarebbe</u>
my intention <u>would be</u>

sia io che mio marito <u>preferiremmo</u>
both I and my husband <u>would prefer</u>

Form

The endings are the same for all verbs:

1st sing	-*ei*	1st plur	-*emmo*
2nd sing	-*esti*	2nd plur	-*este*
3rd sing	-*ebbe*	3rd plur	-*ebbero*

In the first person singular the stress is on the e of the -ei ending, which is regular stress; in the third person plural it is on the -e of the -ebb- syllable, irregular stress, as in the third person of verbs in nearly every tense.

The root is:

– for verbs in the second and third group, the infinitive without the final -e, e.g. **scrivere: scriver-**;
– for verbs in the first group (-are verbs), the infinitive without the final -e but with the -a- becoming -e-, e.g. **parlare: parler-**.

parlare	scrivere	finire	dormire
parlerei	scriverei	finirei	dormirei
parleresti	scriveresti	finiresti	domiresti
parlerebbe	scriverebbe	finirebbe	dormirebbe
parleremmo	scriveremmo	finiremmo	dormiremmo
parlereste	scrivereste	finireste	dormireste
parlerebbero	scriverebbero	finirebbero	dormirebbero

Note: The italic type indicates stress.

Irregular verbs

There are two broad types.

(*a*) Those where the infinitive part of the ending has dropped the first -e- as well as the second and has become shortened to -r-, e.g.

andare – andrei   **avere – avrei**

(*b*) Those where the stem ends in -l- or -n-: in these the **l/n** are replaced by **r**, giving a **double r**:

venire – verrei   **rimanere – rimarrei**

and their compounds (e.g. **prevenire**).

(*c*) Note also:

essere – sarei   **dare – darei**   **dire – direi**
stare – starei   **bere – berrei**

For a full list, see the Grammar reference.

Use

The conditional is used to express the idea: 'I would do', 'we should do', i.e. what would happen if . . . ('conditional' = 'subject to a stated or implied condition').

La mia intenzione <u>sarebbe</u> tornare a risiedere a Milano.
My intention <u>would be</u> to go back to live in Milan.

Implied condition: 'If I manage to get a job in Italy'. Which is also implied in:

Sia io che mio marito <u>preferiremmo</u> abitare in Italia.
Both I and my husband <u>would prefer</u> to live in Italy.

The conditional is often used to soften a statement, make it more polite, as in English.

<u>Vorrei</u> farLe alcune domande.
<u>I should like</u> to put some questions to you (rather than: I want to put some questions to you).

Come <u>giudicherebbe</u> la sua esperienza di lavoro?
How <u>would you evaluate</u> your working experiences?
(rather than: 'how do you evaluate?')

Learners should, as we said in Unit 7, beware of the English word 'would' and not assume it automatically translates by the conditional: it can mean 'used to':

When I was a child I would (= used to) dream of
Quando ero piccolo, sognavo di

Exercise 4

This is what Elisa would do if she were to go back to Italy to live. Fill in the gaps.

Example: (andare) *Andrebbe* a vivere a Milano.

1 (lavorare) _____ nella moda, ma (cercare) _____ un lavoro che non prendesse troppo tempo alla sua vita personale.
2 (preferire) _____ vivere vicino alla sua famiglia.
3 (mandare) _____ il suo curriculum alle più famose case di moda con sede a Milano.

3. The imperative, lei form

The interviewer in Dialogue 1 says:

Ci spieghi
Ci dica

This may look like the present subjunctive, indeed the form is the same. But the interviewer is in fact telling Elisa to do something. It is a command, albeit courteous. Grammatically this is the *imperative*, another mood of the verb (see Unit 4).

Form

As with the present subjunctive, there are just two sorts:

1 -**are** verbs: ending -i
2 all other verbs: ending -a

Verbs which are irregular in the present subjunctive have the same irregular form in the **Lei** form of the imperative.

A useful way to fix the forms in your mind is to think of polite imperatives which are frequently heard, e.g.:

scusi (scusare)
According to the circumstances: excuse me, I am sorry, I beg your pardon

s'accomodi (accomodarsi)
Again, according to the circumstances: take a seat, sit down, make yourself comfortable

venga (venire)
come in, come (here)

dica (dire)
Yes? (said to indicate you are listening) How can I help you?

senta (sentire)
listen, I say (said to attract attention)

Object prounouns with the polite imperative

Object pronouns precede the polite imperative:

<u>Mi</u> scusi!   <u>Mi</u> dica!   <u>S</u>'accomodi!

Note: All examples are translated above.

Exercise 5

The infinitive is often used when giving instructions. But the imperative is also possible. Here are some instructions in the infinitive form. Rephrase them using the polite imperative, as if giving the instructions to a person with whom you have a formal (surname-type) relationship.

Example: **Per cucinare il sugo, <u>seguire</u> queste istruzioni**
Per cucinare il sugo, <u>segua</u> queste istruzioni

1 **sbucciare** e **affettare** una cipolla e uno spicchio d'aglio
2 **lavare** due gambi di sedano e un po' di foglie di basilico
3 **sbollentare** e **sbucciare** un chilo di pomodori
4 **mettere** tutto in una pentola
5 **aggiungere** sale grosso, origano e olio d'oliva
6 **fare** cuocere a fuoco molto basso per un'ora
7 dopo un'ora, **togliere** la pentola dal fuoco e **lasciare** raffreddare il sugo
8 quando è freddo, **passare** dopo aver tolto i gambi di sedano.
Il sugo è pronto.

3. Other imperatives

(*a*) Two plural forms exist:

1. Where the speaker includes him/herself. Form: the 1st person plural of the present indicative of the verb, *never* accompanied by the subject pronoun:

Andiamo!
Let's go.

Vediamo!
Let's see!

2. Where the speaker is addressing two or more people. Form: the 2nd person plural of the present indicative of the verb, again always alone, with no **voi**:

Venite!
Come (here)!

State tranquilli!
Don't worry! (lit.) Be calm!

(b) The informal singular form is not difficult but potentially confusing:

For -are verbs, the ending is: -a

Guarda!	**Scusa!**
Look!	Sorry!
Ascolta!	**Aspetta!**
Listen!	Wait!

For other regular verbs and most irregular verbs, the **tu** form of the verb:

Senti!	**Vieni!**
Listen!	Come!

Irregular are:

essere: sii!   **avere: abbi!**   **dire: di'!**

A few verbs have two possible forms, the 2nd person singular, or an abbreviated version of it:

andare: <u>vai!</u>/<u>va'!</u>	**dare: <u>dai!</u>/<u>da'!</u>**
fare: <u>fai!</u>/<u>fa'!</u>	**stare: <u>stai!</u>/<u>sta'!</u>**

Object pronouns with the imperative

With all except the formal imperative form (see above), object pronouns are attached to the end:

Aspettami!
Wait for me.

Fammi un favore!*
Do me a favour.

Mangiamolo!
Let's eat it.

Dimmi!*
Tell me! (i.e. I am listening to you)

Diteglielo!
Tell him (about it).

*Note: With the abbreviated forms **di'**, **da'**, **sta' fa'**, **va'** the initial consonant of a following pronoun is doubled – in the sound and therefore in the spelling.

Negative imperatives

For all forms except the **tu** form, **non** is placed before the verb.

Non dica così!
Don't say that!

Non andiamo!
Don't let's go!

Non partite ancora!
Don't leave yet!

For **tu, non** + the infinitive is used:

Non partire!   **Non dire così!**

Exercise 6

Your friend is breaking all the regulations on the train. Tell him not to:

Example: **E' vietato fumare. <u>Non fumare!</u>**

1 E' vietato usare la toilette nelle stazioni.
2 E' vietato sporgersi dal finestrino.
3 E' vietato tirare il freno di emergenza.
4 E' vietato mettere i piedi sui sedili.

Dialogue 2

Elisa's interview continues.

Exercise 7

1 What abilities is the company looking for in its interpreters and translators?
2 Elisa thinks she fits their requirements. What reasons does she give to back up her opinion?

D.P.   La nostra ditta si occupa principalmente di import-export con il Regno Unito e con il Nord America. Abbiamo bisogno di interpreti e traduttori che conoscano non solo la lingua inglese, ma che abbiano anche una buona conoscenza della mentalità e della cultura anglosassone, e che siano disposti a viaggiare regolarmente tra l'Italia e il Regno Unito, e tra l'Italia e il Nordamerica. Mi dica in che modo Lei pensa di essere adatta a questo tipo di lavoro.

ELISA   Be' ho vissuto per vent'anni a Londra viaggiando per motivi di lavoro spesso anche a New York dove ho abitato per un paio d'anni. Credo di aver assorbito in tutti questi anni molti elementi della cultura anglosassone e nordamericana. Inoltre mia madre è nata a Bristol, in Inghilterra, e pur avendo trascorso la mia infanzia in Italia, senza dubbio sono stata fin da piccola influenzata dalla mentalità anglosassone.

Vocabulary ♦

anglosassone	Anglo-Saxon – a shorthand for British and North American. The stress falls in -**sass**-.
ho vissuto per vent'anni	Note the use of perfect tense + **per**. Elisa no longer lives there.
viaggiando	A gerund. Note also below:
pur avendo trascorso	although I had spent – more literally: in spite of having spent – a gerund again forming a past: the auxiliary **avere** becomes a gerund, while the main verb **trascorrere** becomes the past participle **trascorso**.

Language points ♦

The subjunctive in relative clauses which describe a type

The employer describes the sort of interpreters the company is looking for:

Abbiamo bisogno di interpreti e traduttori che <u>conoscano</u> ...
ma che <u>abbiano</u> anche una buona conoscenza ... e che <u>siano</u>
disposti
We need interpreters and translators who <u>know</u> ... but who also <u>have</u> a good knowledge ... and who <u>are</u> willing to

The verbs underlined are subjunctives. The clauses containing them can be called adjectival clauses since they act as adjectives, describing the nouns they follow. In a clause where a *type* of person / object etc. is being described, a type which may or may not exist, the subjunctive is used. Compare the sentence above with:

Abbiamo un interprete che <u>conosce</u> bene . . . ma <u>ha</u> anche una buona conoscenza . . . ed <u>è</u> anche disposto a viaggiare.
We have an interpreter who knows well . . . but who also has a good knowledge . . . and is also willing to travel.

In this sentence an actual person is being described, not a type whose existence is hypothetical. When we are in the realm of definite knowledge, of fact, the indicative is used.

Exercise 8

You need someone to reorganise the archives and data your small company holds. Here are the characteristics you are looking for. How will you put them in an advertisement for someone to do this work?

Example: <u>conoscere</u> l'inglese e il francese
Cerco qualcuno che <u>conosca</u> l'inglese e il francese.

1 <u>essere</u> diplomato
2 <u>avere</u> esperienza di lavoro nel settore
3 <u>sapere</u> usare: MS Word, Excel, Access
4 <u>essere</u> disponibile a fare straordinari se necessario

Language learning suggestion

Guessing meaning

Become a word detective, using your existing knowledge to guess meanings. For example, the word **triennale** (Text 1): the Venice Biennale is an art exhibition held every two years; biennials are plants which have a two-year life cycle; **bi-** two, **tri-** three; so **triennale** might be something to do with three years (**anni**).

Using a dictionary

Once you get beyond the elementary level in the study of a foreign language, there is much to be gained from using a defining dictionary, i.e. Italian–Italian. The dictionary we have used for our definitions is known as *Lo Zingarelli*. Details of this and other dictionaries are at the end of this section. A defining Italian dictionary is good for exploring the language and getting a better understanding of what a word actually means. It is also a good way of checking your guessing. For instance:

residence (Unit 1) – *Lo Zingarelli* says:

Complesso alberghiero costituito da piccoli appartamenti completamente arredati e forniti dell'attrezzatura per la cucina.

combinazione – means what you might guess. *Lo Zingarelli* has also:

Caso fortuito, incontro straordinario di fatti e di circostanze: si incontrarono per combinazione; ma guarda che combinazione! Sinonimo: accidente.

The exclamation: **che combinazione!** 'what a coincidence!' is an everyday phrase. Or: **combinazione, l'ho incontrato proprio ieri** – 'by coincidence, I bumped into him yesterday'. **Coincidenza** is not used frequently in this way. Also from the dictionary you will note that the synonym (word with the same meaning) is **accidente**, not **coincidenza** – you have found another 'false friend'.

scorbutico was probably the least guessable word in the list in Unit 4, Exercise 5. *Lo Zingarelli* says:

1. Che (o Chi) è affetto da scorbuto.
2. *(fig.)* Che (o Chi) ha un carattere difficile, bisbetico, scontroso.

The first is a medical term. The second offers a definition of a figurative use of the word. Following up the adjectives **bisbetico** and **scontroso** would enrich your vocabulary.

triennale. *Lo Zingarelli* says:

a Che dura tre anni.   b Che ricorre ogni tre anni.

Give it a try! We list below the most widely found dictionaries. Most are single volume, but one (De Mauro) is a two-volume work. You probably need to handle one or two in order to choose. *Lo Zingarelli* is updated annually so that you will find that its title is no longer 2002.

- *Grande dizionario della lingua italiana moderna*, Milano, Garzanti, 1999 (1 CD-ROM)
- De Mauro, *Il dizionario della lingua italiana per il terzo millennio*, Torino, Paravia, 2000 (2 vols, 1 CD-ROM)
- *Il dizionario della lingua italiana*, Torino, Paravia, 2000 (1 CD-ROM)
- *Lo Zingarelli 2002 con CD-ROM: vocabolario della lingua italiana*, Bologna, Zanichelli, 2001
- Fernando Palazzi, Gianfranco Folena, *Dizionario della lingua italiana*, Torino, Loescher, 1992
- *Dizionario italiano Sabatini-Coletti*, Firenze, Giunti, 1997 (1 CD-ROM)
- Giacomo Devoto, Gian Carlo Oli, *Il dizionario della lingua italiana*, Firenze, Le Monnier, 2000 (1 CD-ROM).

9 La famiglia sta cambiando

In this unit you will

▶ learn more about ways in which Italy is changing, Italian family life in particular
▶ meet **stare** + the gerund – the present continuous tense
▶ meet/revise the future tense
▶ look at the use of **si**, meaning 'one'

Text 1

We heard in Unit 5 how two happy couples met and married. It is widely accepted that the family in Italy is changing. This passage is adapted from an article in the Corriere della Sera *on the 2001 census.*

LA FOTOGRAFIA DELL'ITALIA

21.503.088 FAMIGLIE

Più famiglie, ma più piccole: dieci anni fa erano **19.909.003,** con un numero di componenti medio di **2,8**, sceso oggi a **2,6**

Dove vivono

Nord-Occidentale	6.134.023
Italia meridionale	4.686.957
Nord-Orientale	4.200.634
Centrale	4.170.657
Italia insulare	46.455

Adapted from the *Corriere della Sera*, 28 March 2002

Exercise 1

1 What seemingly odd statistic gives rise to the article?
2 What expression is used for 'single person household'?
3 How would an English text have written the statistic for the average number of children per couple born in Italy?
4 What does the writer say about divorces and separations?
5 She picks out three types of single person household. What are they? And what name does she use which would cover divorced, separated and widowed persons?

Famiglie in aumento e sempre più mini

Crescono le persone che vivono sole per scelta o necessità. Meno figli nelle coppie

Cresce, e di molto, il numero delle famiglie italiane, non cresce invece la popolazione. Ma non è un trucco contabile. E' più semplicemente una rivoluzione culturale e sociale. Perché sono diventate più piccole le famiglie. E sono esplose le famiglie mononucleari: oltre 700 mila in più negli ultimi cinque anni . . .

La verità è che nascono meno bambini, molti meno: in nessuna regione d'Italia si riesce a superare la media statistica di 1,5 figli per donna, nemmeno in Campania che si ferma a 1,43. C'è soltanto un'eccezione: la provincia autonoma di Bolzano che raggiunge il miracoloso 1,52. La media nazionale, però, si ferma a 1,25 bambini per ogni coppia . . . Ma non è soltanto questo. Perché nel nostro Paese continuano anche a diminuire i matrimoni. E a crescere drammaticamente i divorzi e le separazioni.

Ecco perché, alla fine, il nostro Istituto di statistica si trova a registrare un vero e proprio trionfo dei single. Giovani e rampanti. Insoddisfatti e insofferenti. Eterni e irriducibili Peter Pan . . .

Ma nelle cifre dell'Istat ci sono anche i cosiddetti single di ritorno: la valanga di divorziati e separati che affolla le statistiche alla ricerca della stabilità perduta. E tra le famiglie mononucleari bisogna anche fare i conti con quelle famiglie, e non sono poche, formate sostanzialmente da persone anziane. Donne e vedove, per lo più. Sono loro che si trovano molto spesso a viver da sole l'ultima parte della propria esistenza. Perché sono le donne che in Italia si trovano ad avere un'aspettativa di vita ben più lunga dei loro mariti, cinque–sei anni di più, in media.

Alessandra Arachi

Adapted from the *Corriere della Sera*, 28 March 2002

Vocabulary ◆

single di ritorno   Phrase modelled on **analfabeti di ritorno** (**analfabeta** = 'illiterate') used of people who learned to read and write but who, not using their limited skills, have lost them.

per lo più   for the most part. Opposite: **per lo meno**.

Dialogue 1

How do individuals view these changes? Teresa now lives in Britain but she grew up in Naples in the 1970s and 1980s.

Exercise 2

1 Was Teresa's family a large one?
2 What factors made it a 'typical' Neapolitan family?
3 What difference does she expect there to be between the circumstances she grew up in and those she intends for her children, when she has them?
4 What reasons does Teresa give for the fact that couples defer having children?

TERESA   La mia famiglia è una tipica famiglia napoletana . . .
SANDRA   Che cosa vuol dire?
TERESA   Mah, una famiglia dove il padre va a lavorare all'ufficio e la mamma è a casa a cucinare e a badare ai bambini. Penso che sia stata una fortuna per me e mio fratello di avere avuto nostra madre a casa, perché quando ci ripenso e vedo anche come cambia la struttura della famiglia

	moderna . . . sapere che mia madre quando tornavo da scuola era là e potevo stare con lei, è una cosa che certamente ha influenzato molto la mia vita.
SANDRA	E quindi se tu dovessi esprimere un parere sulla famiglia tradizionale italiana . . .
TERESA	E' una famiglia appunto dove il padre va a lavorare, la madre è a casa con i bambini, però so che le cose stanno cambiando e anch'io se un giorno mi sposerò, sicuramente avrò un lavoro e il tempo che potrò dedicare ai miei figli non sarà lo stesso che . . .
SANDRA	Quindi i tuoi amici, a Napoli, che tipo di vita hanno? Sono sposati? Hanno messo su famiglia?
TERESA	Non molti dei miei amici sono sposati perché ci sono molte difficoltà. Quella economica prima di tutto. Trovare il lavoro e quindi i soldi per comprare una casa. Altri amici si sono sposati tardi e aspettano ad avere dei figli . . . aspettano che la situazione economica si stabilizzi . . . perché i figli oggi esigono di più anche a livello economico. Ci sono tante cose che desiderano: il computer, i giochi, cose che forse noi non avevamo e che i genitori oggi si sentono in dovere di fornire ai figli.

Vocabulary ♦

badare ai bambini	to take care of / look after the children. NB: **badare *a* qualcuno, qualcosa.**
se tu dovessi esprimere un parere	if you were to express an opinion. **Dovessi** is an imperfect subjunctive, see Unit 11.
trovare lavoro	Italy has high unemployment, especially in the South where unemployment among the young, even among university graduates, is an especially unhappy problem.

Language points ♦

1. *Stare* + the gerund

You met the gerund in Unit 6. Teresa says:

le cose stanno cambiando
things are changing

To underline that an action/process is ongoing, developing, you can use the gerund with **stare** to form a 'present continuous' in Italian. This is *not* an exact equivalent of the English present continuous.

- In English, 'things are changing' expresses an ongoing process, while 'things change' expresses a generalisation. In Italian, the one word present can express either process or generalisation. Teresa could have said:

  le cose cambiano

  which in English would still in this context be translated 'things are changing'. The choice of saying

  le cose stanno cambiando

  simply underlines the ongoing nature of the action.

- In Italian **stare** + gerund cannot be used to translate the English present continuous used with a future meaning as in:

  Next Friday I am going to London to look for a new outfit for the wedding.

  In Italian, the simple present would be used:

  Venerdì prossimo vado a Londra per cercare un vestito per il matrimonio.

Exercise 3

Complete the following sentences. In certain sentences the only acceptable tense is the simple present. In other sentences both simple and continuous present are correct.

Examples: **Paolo e Francesca (vivere) vivono a Rimini. Francesca (studiare) studia / sta studiando Medicina. Paolo (insegnare) insegna Letteratura Italiana all'Università di Bologna e (scrivere) scrive / sta scrivendo un libro sulla *Divina Commedia*.**

1 Teresa (fare) _____ un dottorato in traduzione letteraria.
2 La settimana prossima Teresa (andare) ____ in vacanza in Italia.
3 Teresa non vuole essere disturbata mentre (lavorare) _____ al computer.
4 Domani Teresa (andare) _____ a trovare un'amica per portarle un regalo di compleanno.
5 Teresa (amare) _____ fare i regali alle sue amiche. Li (comprare) _____ sempre con molte settimane di anticipo.

2. The future

Teresa is unmarried and has a university education. Should she marry and have children in the future, she intends to be a working wife and mother:

> anch'io se un giorno <u>mi sposerò</u>, sicuramente <u>avrò</u> un lavoro e il tempo che <u>potrò</u> dedicare ai miei figli non <u>sarà</u> lo stesso che

Looking ahead in this way, she uses the future tense.

Form

The root for the future is exactly the same as that for the conditional (Unit 8). The endings are the same for all verbs:

1st sing	-ò	1st plur	-emo
2nd sing	-ai	2nd plur	-ete
3rd sing	-à	3rd plur	-anno

giving:

parlare	scrivere	finire	dormire
parler**ò**	scriver**ò**	finir**ò**	dormir**ò**
parler**ai**	scriver**ai**	finir**ai**	domir**ai**
parler**à**	scriver**à**	finir**à**	dormir**à**
parler**emo**	scriver**emo**	finir**emo**	dormir**emo**
parler**ete**	scriver**ete**	finir**ete**	dormir**ete**
parler**anno**	scriver**anno**	finir**anno**	dormir**anno**

Note the stressed vowels at the end of the 1st and 3rd person singular and that the stress in the 3rd person plural is on the penultimate syllable. Note also that the 1st person plural of the future differs from the 1st person plural of the conditional by one letter:

future	*conditional*
scriver**emo**	scriver**emmo**
we shall / will write	we would write

Pronouncing a single or a double **m** makes an important difference in meaning. For irregular verbs, see the Grammar reference.

Use

1. The future can be used to express future actions / states, although the present is used more often than the future. The future tends to be used when there is a hint of hopes, plans which are not yet definite, e.g.

L'anno prossimo <u>vado</u> in vacanza in Grecia.
Next year <u>I am going</u> to Greece on holiday.

with the implication that it is already booked, arranged.

L'anno prossimo <u>andrò</u> in vacanza in Grecia.
Next year <u>I am going to go</u> to Greece on holiday.

with the implication that I intend to go but haven't yet booked.

2. Unlike English, when future events are being referred to, Italian uses the future after time conjunctions e.g. **quando** 'when'; **finché** 'until'; **appena** 'as soon as'; **mentre** 'while'; **dopo che** 'after'; **ogni volta che** 'every time'.

Mi ricorderò questa giornata ogni volta che <u>sentirò</u> quella canzone.
I will remember this day every time <u>I hear</u> that song.

3. The future is used to express a guess, a conjecture, a probability, with no hint of future time being involved. This usage is common.

Suonano alla porta: <u>chi sarà</u>?
The door bell rings: <u>who can it be</u>? / <u>I wonder who it is</u>?

Exercise 4

A group of friends has spent the day in a conference. Now they are about to leave and wonder about the world outside which they have not seen all day. Match up the questions with the English translations.

Example: **1 – e.**

1 Starà piovendo?

2 Saranno ancora aperti i negozi?

3 Farà freddo fuori?

a I wonder if there is a bus service to my hotel.

b I wonder if restaurants are already open.

c I wonder where the taxi rank is.

4 Saranno già aperti i ristoranti?

5 Dove sarà la fermata del taxi?

6 Ci sarà una linea di autobus che va all'albergo?

d I wonder if shops are still open.

e I wonder if it is raining.

f I wonder if it is cold outside.

Dialogue 2

Sylvia asks Lalla about ways in which Italy is changing. Lalla is a grandmother: her elder daughter is married with two children. Lalla is the carer for her grandchildren while her daughter works.

Exercise 5

1 What reason does Lalla give for more women working outside the home nowadays than when she married?

2 How does she sum up family life today as opposed to when she brought up her children?

3 What aspect of the change in family life strikes Lalla as being particularly Italian?

4 She says there is general concern about the low birth rate but what does she deplore?

LALLA   Io penso che la cosa che è cambiata di più è il modo di vivere nelle famiglie. Quando io ero giovane non tutte le donne lavoravano. Molte, quando mettevano su famiglia, stavano in casa a occuparsi dei figli. Oggi una donna che studia vuole metter in pratica quello che ha studiato, e lavora.

Così è cambiato proprio il modo di vivere ... mentre la famiglia prima era il posto che raccoglieva, almeno due volte al giorno, tutti i membri della famiglia, oggi è già tanto se li raccoglie una volta ... è un modo di vivere molto disperso. I membri della famiglia si vedono poco, perché i genitori lavorano fuori casa, i figli stanno nelle scuole ormai a tempo pieno. Quindi hanno poco tempo per stare insieme.

SYLVIA   Chi si occupa dei figli?

LALLA   In parte i nonni, in parte le babysitter e in parte le scuole ... La vita di famiglia secondo me va scomparendo, totalmente.

Eh . . . sì, si vive sotto lo stesso tetto, ma non si fa neanche vacanza insieme, perché sovente i figli vanno uno in vacanza a destra, l'altro a sinistra . . .
Cioè, l'Italia è passata molto velocemente dalla famiglia patriarcale allargata alle famiglie frantumate. Il cambiamento è stato velocissimo.
Tutti gridano che in Italia c'è un decremento delle nascite, che ci sarà un problema per le pensioni eccetera eccetera. Però nessuno protegge queste famiglie. Allora là dove non ci sono dei nonni che aiutano le giovani madri ad allevare i bambini, non ci sono asili nido a sufficienza, le scuole smettono di funzionare al 15 giugno, e ricominciano al 15 settembre . . . e i bambini dove vanno? Allora, è inutile dire che non si fanno figli!
La legge non aiuta le giovani famiglie. Cioè, si dice che bisogna fare una cosa, ma poi non si aiuta a farla.

Vocabulary ◆

mettevano su famiglia	they started a family
tutti quanti	everyone
ormai a tempo pieno	nowadays for a full day. The Italian school day used to run from 8 a.m. to 1.00 p.m. Nowadays many schools operate in the afternoons too.
va scomparendo	This use of **andare** + gerund is similar to **stare** + gerund but with even more emphasis on the ongoing nature of the process.
velocissimo	See Appendix 1.
asili nido	a day nursery. **Asilo** – refuge (cf. asylum); **nido** – nest.
non si fanno figli	people don't have children

Language points ◆

More uses of *si*

Si can be a reflexive pronoun (see Unit 2). But it can also be used as a subject pronoun, somewhat similar to 'one' but much more commonly used. Nor does si sound awkward and aloof, like 'one' in English. Lalla said:

si dice che bisogna fare una cosa, ma poi non si aiuta a farla
they say something should be done but they don't help them do it

Antonio Ricci (Unit 2) said:

si respira aria buona, si guarda il mare, si sta con gli amici
one breathes good air, one looks at the sea, one spends time with friends.

And in Unit 3, Exercise 3, Chiara was asked about life in Siena and answered:

Si fa la vita di una città di provincia . . . si va a teatro
One lives / you live the life of a provincial town . . . one goes / you go to the theatre

1. Si is used in order to speak in a detached, general way rather than attributing to a specific person; in English: 'people', 'they', 'you' or even 'we'. It is sometimes referred to as 'impersonal si' although it is not strictly 'impersonal' but unspecified: 'people in general'. It is not 'it', which, if needed, is esso, essa.

It is possible to use uno rather than si; and also tu. Si is much more common than either.

Spesso in montagna si mangia / uno mangia / mangi la polenta.
You/people often eat polenta in the mountains.

2. Si is also used where English might use a passive (si passivante).

In Italia si produce molto vino.
A lot of wine is produced in Italy.

In Italia, si comprano ogni anno molti computer.
In Italy, many computers are bought every year.

Note: molti computer is plural and is the subject of the verb, which is therefore plural.

3. Note that when si is used with a reflexive verb, third person, so that you get two si, the first becomes ci:

Di solito, dopo avere mangiato, ci si lavano i denti.
After a meal, you usually clean your teeth.

Text 2 ⑩⑨

The Italian family may be changing but a verdict by the Court of Appeal in April 2002 caused some surprise. In Naples, a 30-year-old unemployed law graduate went to court claiming he had a right to financial support from his father until he found work he deemed worthy of his qualifications. The court ruled in his favour. This provoked the following article.

Exercise 6

The writer reports the judgment and comments on the reaction of a psychologist. She then says that in actual fact parents do support their children until they are safely settled. In what ways? She gives three examples.

Vocabulary ◆

sempre che ne abbiano la possibilità economica	provided they are able to financially
la Suprema Corte di Cassazione	the Final Court of Appeal
ricorso	appeal
stufo	fed up
erede	heir. The use of the word has an ironic flavour.
amministratore di una società di famiglia	on the board of a family company (which would mean he would receive some sort of remuneration.)
finché	while, as long as
darsi da fare	to busy oneself, here: to be actively (looking for work)
senza badare a spese	without counting the cost
sarà pure	that may well be
nei fatti	in reality, in actual fact
eventuali bambini	any possible children. **Eventuale** is a false friend: 'in the eventuality that there are some' is how it should be understood.

Figli in casa finché non si realizzano

Obbligatorio per i genitori mantenerli anche se hanno 30 anni

Finché un figlio trentenne non trova il lavoro che gli piace, papà e mamma sono obbligati a mantenerlo, sempre che ne abbiano la possibilità economica. Lo ha deciso la Suprema Corte di Cassazione respingendo il ricorso di un padre napoletano stufo di mantenere l'erede laureato in Legge, intestatario di un fondo di mezzo miliardo e amministratore di una società di famiglia. Mai appagato, però, dalle prospettive di carriera che gli vengono offerte.

Finché la famiglia potrà, e finché il giovane mostrerà di darsi da fare per trovare un ruolo adeguato al suo stato sociale, la famiglia, dice la Cassazione, dovrà provvedere a lui senza badare a spese.

Sarà pure una sentenza che fa discutere, questa. Sarà pure 'diseducativa', come sostiene la professoressa Anna Oliviero Ferraris, docente di Psicologia dell'età evolutiva, perché 'incoraggia la tendenza patologica dei figli a non uscire di casa', a differenza di quanto avviene invece in tutti i paesi del Nord Europa.

Nei fatti, da anni, le cose stanno esattamente come dice la Cassazione. Soprattutto quando la famiglia manda i figli all'università, che pochi, pochissimi studenti finiscono negli anni previsti e molti, moltissimi non termineranno mai.

Quando spera che i suddetti figli troveranno un'occupazione non precaria né flessibile né part-time, per cui servono master e specializzazioni, meglio se conseguite in soggiorni all'estero.

E quando si augura che un giorno questi figli riusciranno ad avere una vita di coppia stabile, in una casa decorosa, con gli eventuali bambini che potrebbero nascere da questa unione.

Simonetta Robiony

Adapted from *La Stampa*, Friday 5 April 2002

ALPI   DOLOMITI

Lago
di Como
Lago
Maggiore
Lago
di Garda

Fiume Po

Mar Adriatico

Mar Ligure   Fiume Arno

Fiume Tevere

Isola d'Elba

Lago
Trasimeno

Isole Tremiti

SARDEGNA

Mar Tirreno

Vesuvio
Ischia
Capri

Mar
Ionio

Stromboli
Isole Eolie
Isole
Egadi

Etna

Pantelleria

Isole Pelagie
Lampedusa

Italy, physical map

10 Nord e Sud

In this unit you will

▶ learn something of the differences between the North and the South of Italy
▶ talk about the way things used to be: revise the imperfect
▶ meet the pluperfect (**trapassato**)

Dialogue 1

The differences between the North and the South of Italy are complex (see Appendix 1). Angelo comes from Calabria, the toe of the Italian boot. Here he recalls his father with admiration: he thinks that had his father lived in the North, his talents and hard work would have made him a much richer man, since running a business would have been less challenging. Nevertheless in a southern context, he was comfortably off.

Exercise 1

1 How did Angelo's father earn his living?
2 He was relatively successful. What in particular does Angelo mention which supports this assertion?
3 What difficulties did he face in running a business?
4 Why does Angelo consider his father was 'wasted' (**sciupato**)?
5 Why were there so many people to feed in the household?

SYLVIA   Suo padre era medico?
ANGELO   No, mio padre era un piccolo industriale del legno e commerciava nel Sud sino a Napoli. Lui forniva delle botti

ai mercantili, per trasportare i liquidi. Faceva delle botti di legno, ma anche altro faceva ... aveva una modesta squadra di quattro o cinque dipendenti. Anche lui però se era necessario lavorava personalmente. Era capace, era molto molto capace. Io sono talmente ammiratore di mio padre che ho detto guarda, un gran personaggio sciupato. Al Nord avrebbe fatto una fortuna sicuramente molto più grande di quella che aveva al Sud. Perché con quei mezzi, con le scarse comunicazioni, col pericolo continuo che incombeva su di lui ... Mio padre era uno dei pochi ad avere una pistola. Due cittadini del mio paese avevano una pistola, e avevano la famosa ... la Colt, no? nella fondina, camminavano sempre con la Colt nella fondina.

SYLVIA   Perché?

ANGELO   Eh, perché c'erano i briganti.

LALLA   Suo padre è nato alla fine dell'Ottocento, perché lui è l'ultimo di dieci figli, quindi si immagini. Si parla di prima della Prima Guerra Mondiale.

ANGELO   E' nato nel 1866 ... e quando doveva prendere il treno per andare a Napoli, per raggiungere la ferrovia dal suo paese doveva fare un dieci–dodici chilometri a piedi ...

SYLVIA   A piedi, addirittura?

ANGELO   Eh, sa, parliamo della fine dell'Ottocento, primi del Novecento. E lì si trattava di passare per delle zone non tanto ospitali, diciamo così. Ecco la necessità di essere armato. E lui viaggiava sempre armato. Sembra strano, ma era un regno da cowboy, sa? E si impegnava talmente ... se no non avrebbe potuto tirare su una famiglia di dodici persone. Perché poi lui ha dovuto lottare anche per i nipoti, perché suo fratello è morto giovane, e ha lasciato sei figli, e mio padre ha dovuto proteggere questi nipotini. Quindi Le assicuro che quando ci si riuniva a casa non erano dodici persone, ma erano venti, ventidue persone. Quindi erano delle tavole immense. Per i tempi in cui viveva lui, riuscire a fare questo, è stato qualche cosa di miracoloso.

Vocabulary ◆

industriale	industrialist (i.e. he had his own business, producing wooden barrels, casks, etc.)
mercantile	merchant ship
mercante	merchant, trader
sino a	= **fino a**, up as far as (meaning Naples was his northern limit. **Sino/fino** are interchangeable, the choice being based on sound, avoiding repetition of the initial consonant, e.g. **sino a Firenze**, **fino a settembre**).
dipendenti	employees (sing: **dipendente**)
guarda	look. This is the '**tu**' form of the imperative. It is here simply a conversational interjection, which you will hear often.
sciupato	wasted, from **sciupare**, which also means: to spoil. (e.g. Sulle coste italiane sono stati costruiti molti alberghi che spesso sciupano il paesaggio.)
i briganti	outlaws, brigands. Brigandago was a largely southern phenomenon, fed by extreme poverty and/or political circumstances (see Appendix 1).
Ottocento	nineteenth century (see Unit 1)
lui	Lalla is referring to Angelo
s'immagini	This is the third person, polite, command form
un regno da cowboy	a kingdom for cowboys, the wild west
zone non tanto ospitali, diciamo così	not very hospitable areas, let's put it like that (understatement)
s'impegnava talmente	he worked so hard
impegnarsi	to commit oneself. The root is **pegno**, a pledge given against one's word.

Language points ◆

Talking about how things used to be: the imperfect tense

Here Angelo is talking about what his father used to do, about the way things were then, before the First World War, as his wife Lalla points out, even back into the nineteenth century, e.g.:

Mio padre _era_ un piccolo industriale.
My father was a small businessman.

Commerciava nel Sud.
He did business in the south.

Forniva delle botti.
He supplied barrels.

Faceva delle botti di legno.
He used to make wooden barrels.

Aveva una modesta squadra di dipendenti.
He had a modest/small team of workers.

Viaggiava sempre armato.
lit. He always travelled armed, i.e. He always carried a gun with
him when he travelled.

He is using the imperfect tense.

Form

The form of the imperfect is not difficult. If you remove the -re from
the infinitive, you have the root. The endings are the same for each
of the three types of verb:

		viaggiare	**avere**	**fornire**
1st sing	**-vo**	viaggia**vo**	ave**vo**	forni**vo**
2nd sing	**-vi**	viaggia**vi**	ave**vi**	forni**vi**
3rd sing	**-va**	viaggia**va**	ave**va**	forni**va**
1st plur	**-vamo**	viaggia**vamo**	ave**vamo**	forni**vamo**
2nd plur	**-vate**	viaggia**vate**	ave**vate**	forni**vate**
3rd plur	**-vano**	viaggia**vano**	ave**vano**	forn*i***vano**

Note: As in many tenses, the stress in the third person plural is irregular and falls on the ante-penultimate syllable – italicised above.

Irregular

1 **essere:** ero, eri, era, eravamo, eravate, *e*rano
2 Verbs with infinitives which are contractions of earlier, longer ones.
   The root is the longer form. The endings, however, are regular:

    dire   (from **dicere** = dice-)   dicevo, dicevi, diceva, dicevamo,
                                            dicevate, dic*e*vano

fare	(from **facere** = **face-**)	facevo, facevi, etc.
bere	(from **bevere** = **beve-**)	bevevo, bevevi, etc.
produrre	(from **producere** = **produce-**)	producevo, etc.

(similar: **tradurre**: traducevo, etc. and all verbs ending in -**durre**, e.g. **condurre, sedurre**)

| **porre** | (from **ponere** = **pone-**) | ponevo, etc. |

(similar: **supporre**: supponevo, etc. and all compounds of **porre**, e.g. **proporre, riporre**)

Uses

It is important to realise that the past tenses in English and those in Italian do not correspond. Italian views the past differently from English. The Latin word which *imperfect* derives from has the meaning: 'unfinished, incomplete'. When the imperfect is used, whether or not the action or event is completed is not the aspect being focused on. Essentially Italian divides the past into:

1 'Events', which took place over a specific period of time, took place once only, and are now finished and are viewed as completed, are expressed in the 'perfect' (**passato prossimo**); i.e. what happened.
2 'Repeated events' or 'habitual actions', for which the 'imperfect' (**imperfetto**) is used; i.e. what used to be done.
3 'Descriptions' of states, situations, people, places in the past – again expressed in the 'imperfect'.
4 'Actions' which were going on at a time in the past, background settings, expressed in the 'imperfect'. There will usually be a contrast between what was going on and an event (see 1) which will be expressed in the perfect. See the examples below (4).

Examples (from the dialogue)

1 Events

Suo padre è nato alla fine dell'Ottocento.
His father was born at the end of the nineteenth century.

E' nato nel 1866.
He was born in 1866.

Suo fratello è morto giovane e ha lasciato sei figli.
His brother died young and left six children.

Mio padre ha dovuto proteggere questi nipotini.
My father had to protect these nephews and nieces.

2 Repeated, habitual actions

Lui **forniva** delle botti.
He used to supply barrels.

Per raggiungere la ferrovia <u>doveva</u> fare un dieci–dodici chilometri a piedi.
To reach the railway (station) he used to have to walk 10–12 kilometres.

<u>Camminavano</u> sempre con la Colt nella fondina.
They always travelled (walked) with their revolver in their holster.

3 Descriptions

Mio padre <u>era</u> un piccolo industriale del legno.
My father was a small-scale industrialist working in wood.

Due cittadini del mio paese <u>avevano</u> una pistola.
Two citizens/inhabitants of my home town had pistols.

Col pericolo continuo che <u>incombeva</u> su di lui.
With the ever-present danger which hung over him.

A casa . . . <u>erano</u> venti, ventidue persone . . . <u>erano</u> delle tavole immense.
At home . . . there were twenty, twenty-two people . . . the tables were huge.

4 Ongoing actions, background settings (not from the dialogue), which were taking place when an event ('perfect tense') happened

Mentre mio padre <u>andava</u> alla ferrovia, è stato aggredito da un bandito.
While my father was going to the railway (station), he was attacked by a bandit.

Mio padre <u>ha comprato</u> una pistola perché <u>doveva</u> viaggiare in zone molto pericolose.
My father bought a pistol because he had to travel through dangerous areas.

Quando <u>avevo</u> dieci anni, mio padre mi <u>ha portato</u> per la prima volta al mare.
When I was 10 years old, my father took me to the seaside for the first time.

Exercise 2

Teresa describes her social life as a young person in Naples. Complete the sentences, filling the blanks with the correct form of the verb indicated. Remember she is describing a past situation (2 above).

Example: **Quando (avere) <u>avevo</u> quindici anni, (vivere) <u>vivevo</u> a Napoli.**

Per quanto mi riguarda, il punto di incontro con i miei amici (essere) _____ la parrocchia. Però (esserci) _____ anche il gruppo che ci (fare) _____ concorrenza che (incontrarsi) _____ al bar vicino alla parrocchia. E non (telefonarsi – noi) _____ per metterci d'accordo, per vederci. (Sapere – noi) _____ che a una certa ora, dopo le sei o le sette, in quel posto specifico (raggrupparsi) _____ il gruppo di amici ... e poi (passare – noi) _____ il resto della serata a chiacchierare, a scherzare, ed (essere) _____ molto bello, è una cosa che adesso mi manca.

Exercise 3

In the box below you will find some past events, followed by an explanation of why the event took place. Match the events with a suitable reason and put the verb into the correct form.

Example: **Paola <u>è andata</u> a casa perché <u>era</u> stanca.**

Paola (andare) a casa		(avere) la febbre
Enrico (non andare) in spiaggia		(volere) salutarlo
Franco e Giovanna (decidere) di sposarsi	perché	(essere) il suo compleanno
Marco (comprare) un regalo per Angela		(non amare) studiare
Filippo (non andare) all'Università		(essere) innamorati
Francesca (telefonare) a Enzo		(essere) stanca

Dialogue 2

People who do not know Italy well often do not realise just how far it is from North to South. Here Lalla talks about the first time she went to visit her husband's family in Calabria, in the early 1960s. The family lived at Cinquefrondi, in the toe of Italy, about half-way between the two coasts, a long journey from Turin even today with motorways (see Appendix 1).

Exercise 4

1 How long did the journey by car take?
2 Why did they not use the motorway?
3 What geographical features of the journey left a particularly bad memory for Lalla?

LALLA   La prima volta che io sono andata in Calabria ci abbiamo impiegato tre giorni, non c'era l'autostrada, bisognava passare per tutte queste strade statali ... Fino a Napoli ancora funzionava, poi dopo quando si cominciava ad attraversare il Cilento ... io lo avevo studiato in geografia ma era una cosa astratta, un punto sulla carta geografica. Il Cilento, farlo in macchina, sulle strade statali, era una cosa da vomitar l'anima, perché sono tante montagne, nessun viadotto, bisognava salire in cima attraverso diecimila tornanti e poi scendere in fondo, poi risalire, poi riscendere, e quando uno diceva: 'Saremo arrivati?' invece c'erano ancora altri cinquanta vallonetti da superare. Quindi era una cosa pazzesca arrivare in Calabria attraverso la Statale.

Vocabulary ♦

strade statali	main roads, other than motorways; not dual carriageways (**superstrade**).
il Cilento	A mountainous area in the south of Campania, the region immediately to the north of Calabria.

da vomitar l'anima	**vomitare l'anima** = to be violently sick. Lalla underlines the nausea induced by so many hills and valleys, twists and turns.
Saremo arrivati?	Can we be there? Have we perhaps arrived? (see Future: Use (3) Unit 9)

Dialogue 3

When Lalla married Angelo, they faced disapproval, not from their families, but from acquaintances in Turin where there was some hostility towards southerners. This was related partly to different ways of life. Sylvia asks about this.

Exercise 5

1 What was the main difference which struck Lalla between the way her family lived and the way Angelo's family lived?
2 In the text find the words for: 'olive press'; 'flourmill'.

LALLA   Ci sono proprio delle differenze, o ci sono state per lo meno, delle differenze grosse, tra Nord e Sud. Penso che in parte adesso le cose siano molto cambiate.

SYLVIA   Le vostre famiglie vivevano in modi molto diversi?

LALLA   Vivevano in modi molto diversi. Quando io sono andata nel '60, nel '61 la prima volta in Calabria, appunto la famiglia di mio marito viveva in un'enorme casa colonica, terreni, eccetera. Era una casa completamente autonoma, cioè loro avevano la terra che produceva, il forno con cui si faceva il pane, gli animali, le galline . . . praticamente non c'era neanche da andare a far la spesa. Avevano il frantoio per le olive, c'era anche il mulino per macinare . . . c'era tutto in quella casa, una casa modernissima . . . tutta ristrutturata, bellissima, piastrellatissima, con impianti ultramoderni, ma la famiglia viveva ancora in maniera . . . come dire . . . in maniera arcaica.

Era molto bello questo, perché la famiglia io l'avevo conosciuta nel primo passaggio alla società, come dire, industriale? . . . da contadini a industriali . . . l'avevo trovato molto affascinante, molto bella questa cosa.

Vocabulary ♦

casa colonica	farmhouse
piastrellatissima	Lalla coins this word herself. **Piastrelle** are tiles, or woodblocks, for flooring. The words **piastrellare, piastrellato** exist. She means the flooring was ultra-modern. She conveys an idea of it being bright and newly done. Adding **-issimo** in this way is frequently done.
impianti ultramoderni	**impianto** = plant, machinery, equipment. Lalla is referring to the plumbing, the electrical installations, the central heating, etc.
primo passaggio	Lalla is conscious of meeting her husband's family just as the change from a peasant society to an industrialised society in Italy began (see Appendix 1).

Language points: the pluperfect tense

The imperfect + participle forms a tense called the pluperfect. It is used to talk about an action in a past preceding that of the imperfect / perfect.

la famiglia l'avevo conosciuta . . .
I had met the family . . .

l'avevo trovato molto affascinante . . .
I had found it very fascinating . . .

Form

finire		uscire	
avevo finito	I had finished	ero uscito/a	I had gone out
avevi finito	You had finished	eri uscito/a	You had gone out
(etc.)		(etc.)	

Use

Exactly as you would expect, as in the English equivalent.

Exercise 6

Complete the sentences by putting the verb in brackets into the appropriate form of the pluperfect:

Example: **A diciotto anni ho trovato il mio primo lavoro a tempo pieno, anche se in un primo tempo (pensare) <u>avevo pensato</u> di fare l'Università.**

1 Quando ho incontrato mia moglie vivevo a Torino, ma prima (vivere) _____ a Padova e a Bologna.
2 (Cominciare) _____ a studiare il russo, però poi ho capito che non mi piaceva e sono passata all'italiano.
3 Lo scorso fine settimana siamo restati a casa, anche se in un primo tempo (decidere) _____ di andare a fare una gita in montagna.
4 Gianni è andato a vedere quel film perché (leggere) _____ sul giornale che si trattava di una storia molto avvincente e che gli attori erano molto bravi.
5 Marco e Bea si sono sposati nel '98, ma (conoscersi) _____ molto tempo prima all'Università, nell' '86.

Language learning suggestions

What are your main interests? Why not try to read about them in Italian? And whether it is soccer or the Italian Renaissance, you should find it easier and more enjoyable to read about than a general topic that means little to you. Moreover you will be acquiring the words you need to talk about it, so that when you meet a fellow enthusiast, you are ready.

11 L'italiano e i suoi dialetti

In this unit you will

- ▶ learn something about Italian dialects and their relation to the standard language of Italy
- ▶ look at the passive with **essere, venire** and **andare**
- ▶ look briefly at more examples of **si passivante**
- ▶ look at word order and style
- ▶ meet some common prefixes
- ▶ meet the imperfect subjunctive

Text

Travellers in Italy usually become aware of local accents and dialects. Some Italians worry that dialects are in danger of disappearing. This prompts suggestions for measures to preserve them such as teaching dialect in schools, a suggestion addressed by the writer of the passage below who is Professor of History of the Italian Language in the University of Turin. (See Appendix 2: Dialects and minority languages.)

Exercise 1

1 Why does Beccaria think Italian needs to be nurtured with care in schools?
2 Why does he consider a mastery of Italian is important to someone living in Sardinia or Friuli?
3 What does he see as the strengths and what as the limitations of dialects?

Professor Gian Luigi Beccaria

4 What practical difficulties would arise if dialects and minority languages were taught in schools?
5 He makes a number of suggestions for ways in which minority languages and their culture can be encouraged in schools. Can you list some of them?
6 Does he think it is important to preserve these localised languages and if so, why?

Non compete alla scuola insegnare i dialetti

L'altro giorno un amico mi chiedeva perché non si insegnavano i dialetti e le lingue minoritarie a scuola. Gli ho fatto notare che noi viviamo in un Paese dove l'italiano come lingua di tutti è una conquista relativamente recente, e che non tutti lo conoscono ancora in modo sufficiente, e che va dunque accudito come un fragile e giovane bene culturale, acquisito da non molto, da coltivare con cura.

Non vedo perché si debbano sottrarre delle ore a scuola per insegnare il piemontese, il siciliano, il friulano o il sardo. Mi sembra poco sensato. La difesa dei dialetti e delle lingue minoritarie va fatta in altro modo, non a scapito della lingua italiana, che è la lingua nostra che dobbiamo saper maneggiare per bene.

E' l'italiano che serve al sardo e al friulano per l'allargamento della propria cultura e per un'apertura sociale. In italiano sono scritti libri e giornali. Il dialetto è un sistema linguistico di ambito geografico e culturale limitato che soddisfa egregiamente, delle nostre esigenze espressive, soltanto alcuni aspetti (l'usuale, il pratico) e non altri (il tecnico, il filosofico, ecc.). Il dialetto lo si parla, in dialetto si comunica magari con maggiore vivacità. Ma si comunica?

E poi, come insegnarlo a scuola? Ci sono alcune difficoltà pratiche. Quale catalano insegnare ad Alghero, e quale varietà sarda in Sardegna, quale albanese nelle colonie? E come si fa ad insegnare lingue che non hanno una norma grammaticale? E poi, ormai i dialetti si sono trasfigurati, mescolandosi con l'italiano, e non esistono più dialetti puri.

Io penso che, per tutelare le lingue minoritarie, è molto meglio a scuola dedicarsi a ricerche d'altro tipo: architettura locale, usi e costumi, credenze, fiabe, leggende, canti, proverbi, inchieste dialettali sulle parole perdute, ecc., offrono spunti infiniti per approfondimenti interessanti, di grande utilità.

E' questo, credo, il modo migliore per salvaguardare le nostre radici culturali e sentimentali. Ed è un compito importante: senza radici l'uomo, oggi più che mai, si perde nell'indifferente, nella purea universale di una cultura anonima dove tutto è uguale a tutto. Dalla perdita delle radici nasce lo spaesamento, lo sradicamento, l'angoscia, malattie del secolo.

Gian Luigi Beccaria

Adapted from: *Supplemento Tuttolibri, La Stampa*, 28 October 2000

Vocabulary ♦

compete	**competere a** to be the duty / task of
le lingue minoritarie	minority languages (several are officially recognised in Italy – see Appendix 2)
conquista recente	See Appendix 2 for a brief historical picture.
un ... bene culturale	The expression is usually applied to artifacts, which form part of the cultural heritage of the country. The Ministry responsible for these is the **Ministero per i Beni Culturali**.
acquisito da non molto	acquired not long ago (note the use of **da**, similar to **acquisito da cinque anni**, acquired five years ago)
da coltivare con cura	to be nurtured with care (a different use of **da**: as in **da non confondere con Capri**. See Unit 2)
poco sensato	not very sensible
sensato	sensible
sensibile	sensitive
a scapito di	at the expense of
per bene	with care, in an orderly way (often written as one word)
libri e giornali	The subject of this sentence – see Word order, below.
egregiamente	exceptionally well
egregio	outstanding
egregio signore	Dear Sir in a formal letter, really means: Distinguished Sir (see also Word order, below).
catalano, albanese	Catalan, Albanian (see Appendix 2)
come si fa ad insegnare	how do you go about teaching (see Unit 9)
mescolandosi con l'italiano	Notice the reflexive pronoun is tacked on to the end of the gerund **mescolando** (see Unit 6).
tutelare, salvaguardare	to preserve, safeguard (often applied to looking after art treasures)

Language points ◆

1. The passive: *è fatto*, *viene fatto*, *va fatto così*

The passive is a verbal form used when the (active) sentence is turned round so that the natural object of the verb is made the subject:

Active:
John fed the cat
John: subject; fed: verb; the cat: object

Passive:
The cat was fed by John.
The cat: subject; was fed: verb: John: agent

'John' is called the agent, and is the natural subject. Sometimes the agent is not expressed:

Jane was seen leaving the cinema alone.
Jane: subject; was seen: verb; agent unexpressed

The passive in Italian is formed with **essere** and the past participle and should not constitute a difficulty to the learner. Any tense of **essere** can be used.

In Italia, il Governo è formato dal Presidente del Consiglio.
In Italy the government is chosen by the Prime Minister.

As opposed to:

In Italia, il Presidente del Consiglio forma il Governo.
In Italy the Prime Minister chooses the Government.

It is, however, also possible to form a passive with **andare** and **venire** and the past participle.

(*a*) **Venire** as auxiliary can be used only in simple (one-word) tenses and has an element of focus on an *action*, whereas **essere** is more related to *state*. They are however to some extent interchangeable:

Il Presidente della Repubblica viene eletto dal Parlamento.
The President of the Republic is elected by Parliament.

Il Presidente della Repubblica è eletto dal Parlamento.
The President of the Republic is elected by Parliament.

(*b*) **Andare** is used as an auxiliary (in the third person singular/plural only) to indicate what should or must be done. As here:

(L'italiano) <u>va accudito</u> come.
Italian <u>should/must be nurtured</u> like.

I dialetti <u>vanno insegnati</u> a scuola.
Dialects <u>should/must be taught</u> in school.

Exercise 2

Instructions to someone who has never flown before. Rephrase these using **andare** + past participle.

Example: **<u>Bisogna allacciare</u> la cintura di sicurezza.**
La cintura di sicurezza <u>va allacciata</u>.

1 <u>Bisogna mettere</u> il bagaglio a mano nello spazio apposito sopra il proprio sedile.
2 <u>Bisogna spegnere</u> il telefonino.
3 Durante il decollo e l'atterraggio, <u>bisogna portare</u> lo schienale in posizione verticale
4 ... e <u>bisogna chiudere</u> il tavolino.

2. Si passivante

The text has several examples of the **si passivante** (see Unit 9):

perché non <u>si insegnavano</u> i dialetti
why dialects <u>weren't taught</u>

perché <u>si debbano sottrarre</u> delle ore a scuola
why time <u>should be taken away</u> (from Italian) at school

il dialetto lo <u>si parla</u>
dialect <u>is spoken</u>

è proprio necessario che lo <u>si scriva</u>?
is it really necessary that it <u>should be written</u>?

Note the order of pronouns: **lo si.**

3. Word order and style

This passage is elegantly expressed and in the third paragraph Beccaria's use of Italian makes his point more effectively. In the first sentence, using:

è l'italiano che serve
it is Italian which is used to

rather than just saying:

l'italiano serve
Italian is used

stresses the word **italiano**, the Italian language, which he has already described as a treasure with the gentle hint that it is on a par with the works of art of which Italy has such a rich store.

Word order is more flexible in Italian than in English. This enables Beccaria to continue to highlight the word **italiano** by inverting the sentence:

Libri e giornali sono scritti in italiano.
Books and newspapers are written in Italian.

Also in the next sentence, the sense is:

Il dialetto . . . soddisfa soltanto alcuni aspetti delle nostre esigenze espressive.
Dialect satisfies only some aspects of our expressive needs.

but the word order enables the writer to be more precise and yet elegant about the needs which dialect does and does not satisfy.

The usage

Il dialetto lo si parla
Dialect is spoken

on the other hand is one often heard: the object of the verb is stated, a pronoun 'repeats' it and then comes the verb. And yet here it is still keeping the structure of highlighting the two media of communication: **italiano** and **dialetto**.

Exercise 3

Reorganise the answer to the question so as to emphasise the object.

Example: **Quando bevi il caffé?**
Bevo il cappuccino la mattina e l'espresso dopo pranzo.
Il cappuccino, lo bevo la mattina. L'espresso, lo bevo dopo pranzo.

1 Dove compri la frutta e la verdura?
Compro la frutta al mercato, e la verdura nel negozio sotto casa.

2 Che tipo di giornali leggi di solito?
   <u>Leggo i quotidiani</u> durante la settimana, <u>i settimanali</u> nel
   weekend.
3 Quando vuoi guardare le foto delle vacanze?
   <u>Guardo le foto</u> adesso, <u>le diapositive</u> con calma, dopo cena.

4. Prefixes

Most of the prefixes commonly used in Italian will not cause difficulty
to English speakers, e.g. **ri** = again:

rifare
to do again / to redo

riaprire
to open again / to reopen

and they will easily recognise the negative prefixes: **dis-** and **im-/in-**:

ordinato / disordinato
tidy / untidy

utile / inutile
useful / useless

It may be helpful to know that **s-** can also be a negative prefix:

spaesamento (from **paese**)
loss of bearings

sradicamento (from **radici**)
rootlessness

cortese / scortese
polite / impolite

leale / sleale
loyal / disloyal

The prefix **stra-** = extra:

pieno / strapieno
full / full to overflowing

cotto / stracotto
cooked / overcooked

Exercise 4

(a) **ri-**

Use the words in the list to make new words with the prefix **ri-** and match them to the English translation.

Example: **leggere** – **rileggere**
to read again, to reread

1 scrivere   a to rediscover
2 pulire   b to reply, retort, contradict
3 scoprire   c to clean up
4 battere   d to write again, to rewrite

(b) **dis-**

You probably know the meaning of the words in bold type; if you don't, look them up. Can you guess the meaning of the words in italics?

Example: **ordinato** (tidy)
disordinato (untidy)

1 **imparare** *disimparare*
2 **informazione** *disinformazione*
3 **attenzione** *disattenzione*
4 **disperare** *sperare*
5 **disabile** *abile*
6 **dire** *disdire*
7 **opportuno** *inopportuno*

(c) **s-**

Answer the questions.

Example: **Sfortunato** means 'unlucky': how would you say 'lucky'? **Fortunato**

1 **Sgarbato** means 'rude': how would you say 'polite'?
2 **Scortese** means 'discourteous', 'rude': how would you say 'courteous'?
3 **Grammatica** means 'grammar': what does **sgrammaticato** mean?
4 **Grasso** means 'fat': what does **sgrassare** mean?
5 **Forno** means 'oven': what does **sfornare** mean?

(d) **stra-**

Complete the sequence.

Example: cooked : **cotto**   overcooked : stracotto

1 full : **pieno**   overfull : _____
2 paid : **pagato**   overpaid : _____
3 to cook : **cuocere**   to overcook : _____
4. to do : **fare**   to overdo : _____

Dialogues

The three dialogues which follow tell you something about different dialects and the Italian language model for the foreign learner.

1. Neapolitan dialect

Sandra asks Teresa whether her family speak Neapolitan dialect.

Exercise 5

True or false:

1 Teresa's grandfather used to play the guitar and sing Neapolitan songs.
2 She is pleased that she can speak Neapolitan dialect.
3 When she was a child she enjoyed speaking dialect outside the home.
4 Speaking dialect was then equated with being a country bumpkin.

SANDRA	Tu, per esempio, il dialetto lo parli, lo capisci?
TERESA	Sì . . . io sono fortunata in questo perché la mia famiglia è una tipica famiglia napoletana anche in questo senso, cioè che parla napoletano . . .
SANDRA	Scusa, i tuoi sono proprio napoletani?
TERESA	Napoletani napoletani. E . . . i miei nonni erano napoletani. Mi ricordo mio nonno che suonava la chitarra, e suonava e cantava queste canzoni napoletane, e si parlava appunto

dialetto in famiglia, per cui in un certo senso mi sento bilingue, e sono contenta. Quando ero ragazzina evitavo di parlare dialetto perché sembrava . . . un problema sociale.

SANDRA Beh, quando noi eravamo piccole in Italia l'idea era che non bisognava parlare il dialetto, è abbastanza recente l'idea che i dialetti sono una ricchezza e bisogna mantenerli . . .

TERESA Infatti . . . non so voi al Nord, ma a Napoli se parlavi il dialetto eri ignorante ed eri una cafona, praticamente. Eri volgare e non c'era quest'idea invece che il dialetto era una lingua, come hai detto tu, piena di ricchezze culturali, insomma una lingua da sfruttare e da conoscere a fondo. E quindi in famiglia appunto parlavo dialetto, però al di fuori con gli amici cercavo di parlare in italiano.

SANDRA Quindi tu il dialetto napoletano lo sai parlare.

TERESA Io il dialetto napoletano lo parlo molto bene.

SANDRA Correntemente?

TERESA Correntemente. Infatti quando non mi ricordo le parole in italiano mi vengono in mente in napoletano. Io il napoletano lo parlo, lo parlo bene. E perciò sono contenta.

Vocabulary ◆

tu il dialetto . . . lo parli?	Note the word order and the use of the pronoun **lo**.
napoletani napoletani	real Neapolitans, very Neapolitan. This doubling to emphasise can be used with adjectives or even adverbs.
cafona	m: **cafone**. A southern word meaning 'farmer', 'peasant' but which has come also to mean 'peasant' with the English pejorative connotation: 'rough', 'ill-mannered'. A regional or dialect word which has been absorbed into standard Italian.

2. Padovano, the dialect of Padua

Padova/Padua is in the Veneto, a proud city with an ancient university which still today enjoys a high reputation. It is not far from Venice and was, from 1405, part of the Venetian Republic. Sandra asks Francesca, who is from Padua and who comes from a family of lawyers, if they speak the Paduan dialect.

Exercise 6

1 What does Francesca see as the difference between Paduan and Venetian dialect?
2 Why does her family not use dialect at home, in her opinion?

FRANCESCA   No, la mia famiglia non parla dialetto. Abbiamo sempre parlato italiano, soprattutto da parte di mio padre che viene da una famiglia dove non si è mai parlato dialetto . . . mentre a casa di mia madre sì, si parlava, però lei con noi non lo usa mai.

SANDRA   Come mai non si parlava il dialetto a casa di tuo padre? Era una scelta della famiglia?

FRANCESCA   Probabilmente . . . A Padova le persone che parlano dialetto vengono identificate come meno istruite. Poi secondo me dipende anche dal fatto che il dialetto padovano è abbastanza volgare, mentre quello veneziano è il dialetto patrizio, dei nobili, e quindi è una lingua che ha anche valore letterario, per esempio Goldoni ha scritto in dialetto. Invece il dialetto padovano viene identificato con la campagna . . . tant'è vero che tante volte si dice: 'Non sa parlare italiano!' Per cui probabilmente il dialetto non era parlato nella famiglia di mio padre perché, siccome era una famiglia abbastanza patrizia, era un modo di distinguersi anche linguisticamente.

E se tu cresci in un ambiente in cui non si parla, non lo parli neanche tu. Lo capisci perché lo senti intorno a te quando esci, per esempio quando vai al mercato, nel centro, allora lo senti, e impari a capirlo, poi ci sono sempre le parole che saltano fuori, anche in famiglia, dialettali.

Vocabulary ♦

il veneziano   See Appendix 2. Venetian dialect
Goldoni   Born Venice 1707, died Paris 1793. Writer of some 150 comedies, which were developed from the **Commedia dell'Arte** tradition in which actors wearing masks improvised on a plot.

3. Sienese dialect

It used to be said that the 'best' Italian was spoken in Tuscany, and in particular in Siena. Sandra, who is from Piemonte, studied for a qualification in the teaching of Italian as a foreign language at the University of Siena. Here she is talking to Chiara, who comes from Siena.

Exercise 7

1 What did the teachers on Sandra's course say about the 'best' Italian?
2 What does Chiara consider is unusual in the area of Siena about the speech of even those who have had little schooling?

SANDRA   Una cosa mi aveva colpito quando ero stata a Siena, dove tutti i formatori erano senesi o toscani. Mi ricordo che noi ci aspettavamo che ci dicessero: 'C'è un certo tipo di italiano che dovete insegnare, che è l'italiano di Toscana'. In realtà loro stessi ci dicevano: 'Non preoccupatevi assolutamente, ormai è accettato che ogni italiano parla un italiano leggermente diverso da quello di tutti gli altri, e non dovete assolutamente cercare di insegnare . . .'

CHIARA   . . . il toscano, insomma! Con la 'c' aspirata!

SANDRA   Mi aveva abbastanza colpita, pensavo: 'Mamma mia! Me lo sta dicendo un senese, e sono a Siena!'

CHIARA   No, quello che penso che abbia il senese, in effetti, è che anche la persona più . . . semplice, va bene?, riesce a parlare utilizzando i verbi . . .

SANDRA   . . . correttamente?

CHIARA   . . . correttamente. Quindi trovi anche la persona molto anziana che lavora nelle campagne che magari declina un verbo . . .

SANDRA   . . . al congiuntivo . . .

CHIARA   . . . al congiuntivo, in modo appropriato. Questa è una cosa che colpisce, magari.

Vocabulary ◆

formatori   (teacher) trainers
congiuntivo subjunctive

Language points ♦

The imperfect subjunctive

Chiara says that around Siena, even country people who had little schooling, use the subjunctive correctly. We introduced you to the present subjunctive. Sandra here uses the imperfect subjunctive:

noi ci aspettavamo che ci dicessero
we were expecting them to say

as she did in Unit 3:

Se tu dovessi descrivere i tuoi fratelli
If you had to describe your brothers and sisters

Form

The root is the same as for the imperfect (Unit 10): remove **-re** from the infinitive.

		viaggiare	**avere**	**fornire**
1st sing	**-ssi**	viaggia**ssi**	ave**ssi**	forni**ssi**
2nd sing	**-ssi**	viaggia**ssi**	ave**ssi**	forni**ssi**
3rd sing	**-sse**	viaggia**sse**	ave**sse**	forni**sse**
1st plur	**-ssimo**	viaggia**ssimo**	ave**ssimo**	forn*i***ssimo**
2nd plur	**-ste**	viaggia**ste**	ave**ste**	forn**iste**
3rd plur	**-ssero**	viaggia**ssero**	ave**ssero**	forn*i***ssero**

Note:

1 The stress is irregular in the 1st and 3rd person plural (the stressed vowel has been italicised above).

2 Verbs which have particular roots in the imperfect (e.g. **fare: facevo**) will have the same root in the imperfect subjunctive (**facessi** etc.)

3 The three verbs which do not conform to this rule are:

    essere: fossi, fossi, fosse, fossimo, foste, fossero
    dare: dessi, dessi, desse, dessimo, deste, dessero
    stare: stessi, stessi, stesse, stessimo, steste, stessero

Uses

1 To express impossible/unlikely conditions. As Sandra did in Unit 3, to say what the consequence would be if something happened. In sentences of this sort, the verb in the 'if' clause is imperfect subjunctive and the verb in the main 'would' clause is conditional:

Se Maria fosse qui, direbbe che siamo pazzi.
If Maria were here, she would say we are mad.

Se vincessi la lotteria, comprerei un pianoforte a coda.
If I won the lottery, I would buy a grand piano.

Vorrei imparare a suonare il piano, se avessi tempo.
I should like to learn to play the piano if I had time.

You will realise this is quite a common type of sentence in everyday talk.

2 The imperfect subjunctive is used in the same circumstances as the present subjunctive (see Unit 4) when the main verb is imperfect, as in:

Noi ci aspettavamo che ci dicessero
We were expecting them to tell us

cf. **Noi ci aspettiamo che ci dicano**
We expect them to tell us

Aspettarsi che is usually followed by a subjunctive: it is expressing an expectation, not a certainty.

Exercise 8

Look at Exercise 3 in Unit 4, p.44. Marta and Gianni have had their blind date but it didn't go as each had hoped. Put all the sentences in the table into the past and finish them as in the example.

Example: **Marta *sperava* che Gianni *avesse* i capelli biondi, *invece aveva i capelli scuri*!**

Language learning suggestion

Don't worry about dialects, accents etc. When you go to Italy, your ear will attune itself to the local accent. There will always be some people who are easier to understand than others, resign yourself to that and practise smiling and asking people to repeat what they said. With people you spend a lot of time with, maybe you can find ways of making them laugh if you need to do it often. But don't be afraid. Our experience is that most Italians are patient with foreign learners of Italian because they are pleased that the learner is making the effort to learn their language.

12 Essere italiani

In this unit you will

▶ look at further aspects of Italian life and the Italian
character
▶ meet the past definite (**passato remoto**)
▶ look at relative pronouns
▶ meet some more 'false friends'

Text 1

*The bar is very much part of everyday life in Italy. Italians consider
the coffee made in bars the best and they usually drink it standing
at the counter. The idea that the Americans can improve on the bar
as they know it seems somewhat improbable and therefore amusing
to them.*

Exercise 1

1 Passarini is not convinced, 100 per cent, that Starbucks will
succeed in Italy. What word indicates this?
2 What seems to be Howard Schultz's opinion of American
coffee? And of the way it was served?
3 Passarini underlines a number of differences between a
Starbucks café and an Italian bar, mocking the American
version as he does so. What differences does he comment on?
4 In the last paragraph Passarini implies that Starbucks
may well be necessary in other countries but not in Italy.
Why?

L'espresso made in Usa sbarca in Italia 'Starbucks camliera le alitudini'

IL PRIMO BAR
La "Bottega del caffè" è nata a Venezia nel 1640

LE MISCELE
Le migliori sono **arabica, robusta, liberica** ed **excelsa**

CONSUMI
5 chili a testa ogni anno (gli italiani sono undicesimi nella classifica mondiale: ai primi tre posti Svezia, Norvegia e Finlandia)

TAZZINE AL GIORNO
Fino a tre: **81%**
Fino a sei: **15%**
Più di sei: **4%**

I MODI
- *Espresso*
- *Cappuccino*
- *Con limone*
- *Con panna*
- *Al vetro*
- *Corretto*
- *Americano*
- *All'orzo*
- *Macchiato*
- *Freddo*
- *Leccese*
- *Con cacao*
- *Decaffeinato*
- *Shakerato*

UNA PASSIONE NAZIONALE

DOVE
A casa: **70%**
Al bar: **16%**
Al distributore automatico: **14%**

QUANDO
Al mattino: **75%**
Al pomeriggio: **22%**
Durante il giorno: **3%**

Come vendere vasi a Samo, direbbe un bravo professore di liceo. Eppure Starbucks ci proverà: a vendere l'espresso, il suo espresso americano, agli italiani. Dal quartier generale londinese, Mark McKeon, presidente di Starbucks Europa, Medio Oriente e Africa, conferma che, 'entro la fine del prossimo anno', saranno aperti negozi in Germania, Francia, Spagna e, come si diceva, Italia. Sarà.

In ogni caso, sarebbe un errore sottovalutare il gigante nato una trentina di anni fa a Seattle. Howard Schultz, il fondatore, fece in realtà un'operazione molto semplice. Andò in Italia e venne conquistato dai suoi bar, dall'espresso e dal cappuccino invece dei beveroni americani in bicchieroni di 'styrofoam'; dall'informalità dell'ambiente e dal bancone.

Naturalmente Schultz fornì la sua interpretazione del bar italiano, con estremizzazioni e compromessi. Così, chi entri in uno Starbucks, diciamo, di Washington ('no smoking' di rigore) nota le seguenti cose: la gente ordina cose inaudite, come un 'mochacinou' (cappuccino fatto con la Moka). Oppure contorce la lingua per un 'caffèi con lachei', o magari per un 'expresou solou' (esiste anche il 'doppiou') o per un 'ristretou'. Tutto questo mentre, nonostante l'esistenza del bancone, gli avventori stanno rigorosamente in chilometrica e disciplinata fila indiana per ore, attendendo che disorientati baristi producano la schiuma del 'capusinou' con l'aria di praticare un rito woodoo.

Tra le cose non italiane di questi bar c'è una certa accuratezza nel servizio e un ordine che aiuta la chiacchiera e la lettura. L'Espresso-Bar reinventato è congeniale agli anglosassoni. In Italia, il pensiero dell'arrivo di Starbucks può far sorridere, dal momento che il bar 'è' italiano. Ma non è comunque un buon segno quando si hanno molti imitatori?

Paolo Passarini

Adapted from: *La Stampa*, Wednesday 4 April 2001

Vocabulary ♦

vendere vasi a Samo	to carry coals to Newcastle
entro la fine del prossimo anno	by the end of next year
entro venerdì	by Friday
beveroni	*Lo Zingarelli* has two meanings for **beverone**: 1. *Bevanda per le bestie, composta d'acqua e farina o crusca* 2. *Bevanda abbondante insipida.*
chi entri	**chi:** the person who. Subjunctive – a type of person (see Unit 8).
nonostante il bancone	Italians do not queue at the bar: they spread out along the bar counter and try to catch the barman's attention. The implication is that Starbucks has a bar which would allow for this, so why queue?

fila indiana	single file. You sometimes have to queue at the cash desk to pay in an Italian bar – and you do this before you order – but the queue is just a crowd of people around the till rather than a line. And after that you will have to make eye contact with the barman in order to establish your turn.
disorientati	disorientated, not knowing quite what they are doing. Italian barmen on the other hand usually have great skill and produce the coffee with corresponding nonchalance and flourish.
accuratezza nel servizio	probably referring to the little courtesies that Americans in service industries are so good at.
dal momento che	since

Language points ◆

The *passato remoto* (past definite)

The writer recounting the history behind Starbucks uses a different past tense, a one-word tense:

Howard Schultz . . . <u>fece</u> . . . un'operazione molto semplice.
<u>Andò</u> in Italia e <u>venne</u> conquistato dai suoi bar . . . Schultz
<u>fornì</u> la sua interpretazione

This is the **passato remoto** or past definite.

Form

	parl**are**	vend**ere**	forn**ire**
1st sing	parl**ai**	vend**ei** (-**etti**)	forn**ii**
2nd sing	parl**asti**	vend**esti**	forn**isti**
3rd sing	parl**ò**	vend**è** (-**ette**)	forn**ì**
1st plu	parl**ammo**	vend**emmo**	forn**immo**
2nd plu	parl**aste**	vend**este**	forn**iste**
3rd plu	parl**arono**	vend**erono** (-**ettero**)	forn**irono**

Note:

- You will, if you look carefully, see the endings are similar but each type of verb has the characteristic vowel (a, e, i).

- The stress in the 3rd person singular is on the final vowel, which is written with an accent to show this; note also: as in many tenses, in the 3rd person plural the stress falls on the antepenultimate syllable (two before the last)

- The 2nd group has commonly used alternative forms.

- Many verbs are irregular in this tense; verbs in the 2nd group particularly. There is a list of common irregular past definites in the Grammar reference. The most common irregular ones are listed below.

- **Andare**, which appeared in the text and examples, is regular in this tense.

Common irregular verbs:

essere:	fui, fosti, fu, fummo, foste, furono
avere:	ebbi, avesti, ebbe, avemmo, aveste, ebbero
venire:	venni, venisti, venne, venimmo, veniste, vennero
dire:	dissi, dicesti, disse, dicemmo, diceste, dissero
conoscere:	conobbi, conoscesti, conobbe, conoscemmo, conosceste, conobbero

Use

In northern Italy this tense is little, if ever, used in speech; in central and southern Italy it is. It is usually used to recount events which are over and done with, no longer having any link with the present. This is the case with story-telling so that when someone is telling you a story, they may use the past definite. It is also usually the narrative tense in print, i.e. in novels, history books, etc. It is not usually used by journalists recounting events, which often, of course, still have a psychological link to the present.

The foreign learner can safely use the **passato prossimo** when talking about past events. They will need to be able to recognise the **passato remoto** if they want to read novels etc.

The past definite interacts with the imperfect in the same way as the perfect (see Unit 10).

Chiara and Claudio

Exercise 2

Chiara who is from Siena, in central Italy, told Sandra how she married Claudio and where they lived. She used the past definite. We have omitted the verbs. Put them in, using the verbs in the list – they are not in order and you may use each of them more than once. The first one is done as an example.

> decidere   fare   laurearsi   conoscere   chiamare
> rimanere   lavorare   avere

Quando io <u>mi laureai</u>, (1) _____ Claudio. Lui lavorava all'Università come ricercatore. Lavorava con delle borse di studio. Lui aveva questo desiderio di andare negli Stati Uniti per fare ricerca, perché indubbiamente è il posto dove si lavora meglio in questo campo. (2) _____ la possibilità di andare in Texas, a lavorare, e allora (3) _____ di sposarci e di andare insieme. Io (4) _____ come 'visiting scientist' in un laboratorio per tre anni. Poi mi (5) _____ dall'Università di Siena per dirmi che c'era la possibilità di un dottorato di ricerca. Io avevo desiderio di tornare in Italia, e quindi (6) _____ di partire mentre Claudio (7) _____ in America a lavorare per un altro anno. E lui là durante quel periodo (8) _____ il suo PhD.

Text 2 🔊

Raffaella Silipo writes on theatre and cinema for La Stampa. *We asked her to write a short article on Italian cinema.*

Exercise 3

1 Silipo starts by saying there are two views of Italian cinema. What are they?
2 She says after years when there were either intellectual films of limited appeal or rather heavy-handed comedies, a new type of film is emerging. How does she characterise it?
3 Sergio Castellitto and Stefania Rocca are actors. What qualities do they have according to the writer?
4 What are the themes of the new type of film?
5 What does Silipo feel happens to Italian films outside Italy?
6 Some connoisseurs, in France particularly, like another type of Italian film. What is it?
7 Silipo comes to a regretful and regrettable conclusion. What is it?

La doppia vita del cinema italiano

Il cinema italiano? In Italia è una cosa, visto dall'estero è un'altra. In Italia, infatti, dopo anni di schizofrenia – da una parte i film snob, intellettuali, dall'altra le commedie grevi dei comici – si sta affermando un filone vitale: sono arrivate nelle sale con buon successo alcune commedie leggere ma con stile.

Giovani registi come Gabriele Muccino, che con il suo *L'Ultimo Bacio* ha battuto record d'incassi mai visti prima. Attori bravi e non gigioni come Sergio Castellitto, applauditissimo al Festival di Cannes con *L'ora di religione* di Marco Bellocchio. Attrici che puntano sull'intensità e sull'intelligenza prima che sul fascino, come Stefania Rocca, che ha avuto un successo personale in *Casomai* di Alessandro D'Alatri. I temi sono spesso intimisti, crisi di coppia o di famiglia, ma non mancano le opere più impegnate, come *I cento passi* di Marco Tullio Giordana, storia di un delitto di mafia negli anni '70: un gran bel film di denuncia che descrive una Sicilia e un'Italia non stereotipata, non da *Padrino* per intendersi. Anzi, prende in giro la macchietta del mafioso che intona 'Volare ooo' e tanto piace all'estero.

Ecco la doppia vita del cinema italiano: un film come *I cento passi* è stato scartato per l'Oscar, premio che invece è stato vinto da un'opera come *Nuovo Cinema Paradiso* di Tornatore, storia di un ragazzino povero in un Meridione che sembra uscito da un acquerello. Lo stesso Sud Italia che si ritrova in *Il postino*. Sono film molto curati dal punto di vista estetico, con bei paesaggi tradizionali, sole e mare, e protagonisti stereotipati: il bambino magro magro con gli occhioni neri, la Maria Grazia Cucinotta bruna, bella, prosperosa e pessima attrice, che non a caso è una delle nostre poche dive 'da esportazione'.

Ma pensiamo anche a *Mediterraneo*, altro Oscar italiano di Gabriele Salvatores, dove i nostri soldati hanno la faccia latina di Diego Abatantuono e pensano agli spaghetti più che a combattere. Oppure – per altri versi – a *La vita è bella* di Roberto Benigni, un film esile con una tesi molto discutibile sull'Olocausto, premiato con l'Oscar per la recitazione. Benigni è in effetti uno straordinario attore, una maschera della Commedia dell'Arte, però come molti nostri comici eccede nel regionalismo e rischia di trasformarsi in macchietta.

All'estero, soprattutto in Francia, è comunque apprezzato anche il cinema intellettuale, raffinato ma richiuso su se stesso, molto generazionale, di sinistra, di cui alfiere è Nanni Moretti. Un cinema che non ha mai fatto molti incassi ma è amatissimo dal pubblico d'essai. Insomma, piace l'Italia della macchietta o quella degli intellettuali. L'Italia vera, controversa, profonda, quella non interessa a nessuno.

Raffaella Silipo, Vice Capo, Servizio del Settore Spettacoli, *La Stampa*

Written for *Colloquial Italian 2*

Vocabulary ♦

schizofrenia	The writer uses this word to sum up the dichotomy she saw in the cinema in Italy until recently: intellectual films on the one hand with limited appeal, and heavy-handed comedies on the other.
greve	heavy
gigione	Said of an actor who overacts in order to draw attention to himself.
impegnate (f.pl.)	(here) committed politically, with a social message
macchietta	caricature
anzi	on the contrary
'volare ooo'	*Volare* was a 1960s hit song. The refrain goes: *Volare, oh, oh, . . .cantare, oh, oh, oh, oh . . .* Ask any Italian, they'll sing it for you!
prende in giro	it makes fun of
prosperosa	shapely, curvaceous
alfiere	standard bearer, leader
pubblico d'essai	audiences who like avant-garde cinema
Il cinema d'essai	experimental cinema

Language points ♦

Relative pronouns: 'who', 'which', 'that', etc.

These are fairly straightforward in Italian.

1. They must not be omitted, whereas in English they sometimes can be:

> Lo stesso Sud Italia <u>che</u> si ritrova in *Il postino*
> The same South Italy one finds in *Il postino*

2. **Che** can stand for both people and things (i.e. the animate and the inanimate); be singular or plural; and be subject or object of the

verb which follows; in other words it means: who, whom, which, that, or indeed English may not translate it at all (see 1. above):

Gabriele Muccino _che_ con il suo _L'Ultimo Bacio_ ha battuto record d'incassi mai visti prima (animate, subject, singular)
Gabriele Muccino <u>who</u> with his _The Last Kiss_ beat all records for takings

attrici _che_ puntano sull'intensità e sull'intelligenza (animate, subject, plural)
actresses <u>who</u> aim at intensity and intelligence

un gran bel film di denuncia _che_ descrive una Sicilia e un'Italia non stereotipata (inanimate, subject, singular)
a really good accusatory film <u>which</u> describes a Sicily and an Italy which are not stereotypes

il film _che_ abbiamo visto domenica ha vinto un premio a Cannes (inanimate, object, singular)
the film we saw last Sunday won a prize at the Cannes festival

3. **Chi** has a very restricted use; it means 'those who, people who':

chi entri in uno Starbucks
<u>anyone</u>/<u>people who</u> go(es) into a Starbucks

It means: 'who?' only when asking questions (see Unit 4).

4. **Cui** has the same meaning as **che** but is used after a preposition.

per i tempi _in cui_ viveva lui
(Unit 10 – Angelo referring to his father)
for the times he lived in (<u>in which</u> he lived)

per cui is frequently used to mean: therefore, so (on account of which)

si parlava dialetto in famiglia, _per cui_ in un certo senso mi sento bilingue (Unit 11 – Teresa talking about Neapolitan dialect)
we spoke dialect at home, so in a way I feel bilingual

5. **Cui** can be replaced by **il quale, la quale, i quali, le quali** which have the advantage of showing gender and number and may be preferred on that account. They are used in writing; in speaking they sound pedantic.

Exercise 4

Italian actors, actresses and directors

Look at the photos on p. 157 of some Italian actors and actresses. Read the description, translate it into Italian and match it with the right photo.

> Example: The man who is performing in front of a microphone is the actor and director Roberto Benigni.
>
> **L'uomo che sta recitando davanti a un microfono è l'attore e regista Roberto Benigni.**
>
> (Personaggio A)

1 The young woman who is wearing a black dress is the actress Maria Grazia Cucinotta.
2 The man who is shielding his eyes from the sun is the director Marco Tullio Giordana.
3 The man who is smiling, with a beard and a sun tan, is the actor Diego Abatantuono.
4 The young woman who is crossing her arms on her chest is the actress Stefania Rocca.
5 The man who is sitting down and clapping his hands is the actor and director Nanni Moretti.

Exercise 5

Italian films

Translate from Italian into English:

> Example: **Il film di cui ti sto parlando ha vinto l'Oscar.**
> The film I am talking to you about has won an Oscar.

1 L'attrice a cui hanno dato il ruolo della protagonista in *Casomai* si chiama Stefania Rocca.
2 Roberto Benigni è un attore italiano a cui hanno dato un premio Oscar pochi anni fa.
3 *Nuovo Cinema Paradiso* è un esempio di film in cui ci sono molti stereotipi italiani.
4 *I cento passi* è un film con cui Marco Tullio Giordana ha voluto denunciare la mafia.

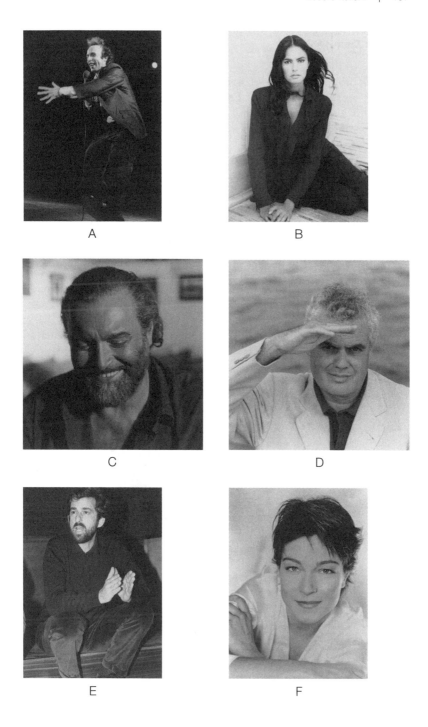

A

B

C

D

E

F

Text 3 🔊

Raffaella Silipo talked about stereotypes of Italians and the real Italy. So we e-mailed a teacher of English in Italy, Angioletta Viviani, to ask her, as an Italian, a Tuscan, what being Italian meant to her. Her reply is opposite.

Exercise 6

What do the following words mean? Choose the correct response from the three suggested. If you don't understand the definitions, use a dictionary. You will find an explanation in English in the Vocabulary for the Text.

1 una persona geniale è: a una persona molto allegra e divertente
                                      b una persona molto intelligente
                                      c una persona molto pigra
2 una disgrazia è: a un avvenimento tragico e sfortunato
                                        b una cosa di cui vergognarsi
                                      c. uno svenimento

Angioletta and her husband

Da: Angioletta Viviani

Data: 20 luglio 2002 18:05

A: Sylvia Lymbery

Oggetto: Cosa significa essere italiani oggi?

Allega:

'La ringrazio per questa interessante e bella domanda', come dicono i politici per prendere tempo prima di rispondere ad un quesito molto difficile e imbarazzante.

Beh, si possono avere sentimenti contrastanti e tormentati, a questo proposito.

C'è la rabbia che ti prende quando, nel traffico cittadino o in autostrada, vedi qualcuno zigzagare pericolosamente per guadagnare pochi metri di vantaggio su di te, o quando senti lodare e vedi rispettare i *furbi* che sono riusciti ad ottenere ricchezza e promozione sociale senza tanti scrupoli. Oppure quando rifletti sul talento di concepire ottime leggi, ma allo stesso tempo sull' incapacità degli italiani di rispettare le regole anche meno impegnative, come il divieto di fumo nei luoghi pubblici o l'obbligo delle cinture di sicurezza (a proposito, solo il 20% le indossa!). Allora puoi addirittura pensare dentro di te a lasciare questo Paese che ti fa tanto arrabbiare e emigrare altrove; e cominci a passare in rassegna le nazioni che conosci meglio e quasi decidi di trasferirti per sempre . . . dove? In . . . Francia, Inghilterra, Stati Uniti?

Ma poi, qualche volta, improvvisamente pensi a tutto quello che gli italiani hanno fatto nel passato e riescono a fare anche adesso, superando tutti gli impedimenti che incontrano. Rifletti sul successo che l'Italia ha nei più svariati campi, pensi ai grandi architetti di oggi, agli stilisti dotati di eccezionale creatività, ai ricercatori scientifici che senza molti mezzi riescono a progredire e a fare nuove importanti scoperte, ti vengono in mente registi e attori geniali, grandi costruttori di Formula Uno, musicisti di talento e tanto altro ancora. Senti una specie di orgoglio crescere dentro di te e, se sei in giornata buona e non hai ancora avuto la disgrazia di incontrare qualche *furbo*, giungi addirittura a chiederti se esista un genio esclusivamente italiano.

Vocabulary ♦

furbi	people who are clever at taking advantage of situations for their own benefit; crafty, cunning
sono riusciti ad ottenere ...	have succeeded in obtaining. Note: **riuscire a fare** – in English to succeed in doing
promozione	advancement
divieto di fumo	Which is one reason why Passarini wonders how Starbucks will fare in Italy.
passare in rassegna	to review (a military expression)
superando tutti gli impedimenti	overcoming all the obstacles. **Furbizia** (being **furbo**) is something which is very close to another Italian skill: **l'arte dell'arrangiarsi** – managing in difficult circumstances. It has been argued that the need to hone this skill is part of the key to what Viviani calls: **genio esclusivamente italiano**.
geniale	brilliant, of genius (not **genial**: it is a false friend – see below, Language points).
disgrazia	(here) piece of bad luck. Also: accident, misfortune (not disgrace: another false friend)

Language points ♦

E-mail

The word 'e-mail' has been adopted into Italian. The system for electronic mail is usually considered feminine. A message (an e-mail) can be either: **un e-mail** or **un'e-mail**. It is often abbreviated to **mail,** often feminine: **una mail.** Such transformations sometimes happen to borrowed words.

False friends / *falsi amici*

We have pointed some of these out to you in the course of this book so you will be familiar with the term and will understand that they are words which look similar in Italian and English but which are used differently in the two languages. Keep an eye out for them and above all, try to use them correctly. Indeed concentrating on the areas where the two languages differ, in structure too, can help to make your Italian more and more convincing. Enjoy the compliments you will surely get.

Language learning suggestion

May we just say: don't stop here! We haven't explained everything in this book. Perhaps you will find it profitable to come back to it in a year or so. But meanwhile look at other courses, even beginners' courses. Almost always you will find something new, something which makes difficult points clearer, possibly just words you didn't know. Keep on working at your Italian, gradually you will get better and better; and it will give you more and more satisfaction and pleasure. **Coraggio e 'in bocca al lupo'!**

Appendix 1 Background

This appendix contains background information to some of the passages in the book. It is not intended to be a comprehensive treatment of the topics it covers but rather to flesh out and make more comprehensible references in the various texts.

History

Italy as a nation is relatively young. Unification dates from 1860, with the Veneto being added in 1866 and Rome in 1870. The country had been largely united under the Napoleonic conquest (1796–1814) but before that, since Roman times, the peninsula had been a series of separate states, the number and composition of which varied over time. Particularly notable were:

- The Republic of Venice, la Serenissima, which boasts a 1,000-year history ended by Napoleon. During the thirteenth to fifteenth centuries it controlled much of the eastern Mediterranean and by the end of the fifteenth century such was its power that it was feared by other European states which successfully checked it.
- Florence, first a republic, then under the Medicis, the Grand Duchy of Florence and later of Tuscany, was immensely rich at the height of its power and, in the late Middle Ages and in the Renaissance (fourteenth to sixteenth centuries), an outstanding cultural centre.
- The Papal State, with the Pope as its temporal ruler and Rome its capital, controlled various parts of central Italy from the eighth century until 1870 when it became part of the new Kingdom of Italy.
- The Kingdom of the Two Sicilies, whose capital was Naples, was formed in 1816 at the end of the Napoleonic period. It was made up of a large part of southern Italy and Sicily, covering some very difficult terrain (see below), and was ruled by a descendant of the Spanish Bourbon family which had ruled the Kingdom of Naples in the eighteenth century as well as the Duchy of Parma and Lucca in the North. Essentially feudal in character, in spite of

some attempts at modernisation, it was less prosperous than more northerly states. Partly because of the terrain and poor communications, the influence of the state was remote for many inhabitants.
• Other smaller states also had their periods of fame.

The mid-nineteenth-century move for unification, the Risorgimento, came largely from the Kingdom of Sardinia, a constitutional monarchy, whose capital was Turin. Its ruling house, the House of Savoy, became kings of the new state (proclaimed in 1861), the first king of Italy being Victor Emmanuel II (he was the second Victor Emmanuel to be king of Sardinia). The first capital of the new state was Turin. The king and parliament moved to Florence five years later and to Rome in 1870.

After the unification of Italy and the fall of the Bourbon king of Naples (1860), brigandage increased in reaction to the introduction by the new state of military service and the imposition of heavy and more efficiently collected taxes. Little account seems to have been taken of poverty or indeed of the fact that many people in rural areas rarely used money. Brigandage was for a time also fostered by the former king with the intention of regaining his throne. This is the period Angelo refers to in Unit 10.

Following the Fascist period (1922–43) and the end of the Second World War, during which Italy was fought over, the Italian people voted to become a republic in a referendum of 1946. The constitution, drawn up by a Constituent Assembly, came into force on 1 January 1948. Its first article is: **L'Italia è una Repubblica fondata sul lavoro** 'Italy is a Republic founded on work'.

Social change

And work was at the heart of the changes during the 1950s and the 1960s. Italy moved from being a predominantly agricultural economy at the end of the Second World War to a modern industrial economy. Its industrial revolution was accomplished in a very short period of time and by the late 1980s Italy was claiming to have overtaken Britain as the fifth largest economy among western industrialised countries. It has not held on to this position but is certainly in the top ten.

There had been flourishing areas of industry before the Second World War, notably the triangle Milan – Turin – Genoa. In the 1950s industry, producing consumer goods such as cars and domestic machines, grew dramatically, needing more and more workers. In rural Italy many people were living at subsistence level, many were underemployed or unemployed and poverty was widespread. People therefore began to leave the land in ever increasing numbers, flocking from the South and the then poor North-East to the cities of the 'Industrial Triangle', while in the Centre, areas like Tuscany, Umbria and Emilia Romagna, the movement tended to be from the land to the nearest large city. This 'Esodo Rurale', flight from the land, made the Italian 'Economic Miracle' possible. It brought to many, if not most, a very different way of life and a prosperity never before dreamed of. Lalla (Unit 10) was indeed witnessing an important historical moment. As a result of the industrial success, the economic well-being of most Italians changed out of all recognition in the second half of the twentieth century.

Another change which stands out in Italy is in the area of the family. There has been a sharp reduction in family size, something which usually goes hand in hand with growing prosperity. The birthrate in Italy is now the lowest in Europe; Italy is not reproducing itself. The overall population figure stays roughly the same because of the number of immigrants. This has meant a historic reversal: traditionally Italy has been a country of emigrants.

The status of women has also changed fundamentally, with the reform of family law in 1975. This gave the two partners in a marriage parity and rewrote the relationship between parents and children, making it less authoritarian. The family is undoubtedly a central institution in Italian life, with far-reaching links to the way the economy and much else functions. But as Lalla says (Unit 9) the way the family lives is changing. One wonders whether it will change the family's importance in society.

Political change

The Italian economic miracle of the 1950s and 1960s did not happen without social tensions: one aspect of this was hostility on the part of many northerners to the southerners flocking north, which Lalla talks about in Unit 5. In more recent years the economy of the North-East which was initially not part of this boom has taken off and it is now the most prosperous area in the country. The changes appear to be behind the rise of various mainly right-wing regional autonomy movements in the North, the most notable being the Liga Veneta and the Lega Lombarda. In 1991, the various leagues fused to form a northern political party, the Lega Nord. It demanded regional autonomy, taxes collected and spent locally, and a regional basis for administration. It sees the North as dynamic, hardworking and efficient and the South, Rome included, as living off the North's hard-earned money.

Another important political change in recent years is the exposure in the early 1990s of the corruption in the political parties which had governed Italy since the war and their subsequent collapse. This has led to changes which seem to allow 'alternanza' in government, with two broad groupings alternating power between them, as opposed to the same grouping holding on to power, as had been the case for forty years. A grouping of left-wing parties, brought together by Romano Prodi, held power for the first time ever between 1996 and 2001. At the time of writing, following the elections of 2001, the government is a right-wing coalition. The main party is Forza Italia. This was founded by Silvio Berlusconi following the collapse of the governing parties. At the time of writing he is in his second term of office as Presidente del Consiglio (Prime Minister), the first having been from March to December 1994. Also represented in the government are members of Alleanza Nazionale, led by Gianfranco Fini. He formerly led the Movimento Sociale Italiano, the successor of the outlawed Fascist Party. The MSI split and Fini formed Alleanza Nazionale, a grouping of the more moderate elements which has rejected all links with Fascism. Also in the governing coalition is the Lega Nord, as agreed before the election, although the Lega saw a big reduction in its share of the votes at the 2001 election. It would be rash to attempt to guess how the overall situation will develop.

North–South differences

The differences between North and South have been a subject of discussion for at least a century. They are complex and include geographical and historical factors. The historical factors include the way the various parts of Italy have been governed throughout the last two thousand years. It should not be forgotten that in parts of Italy, notably the Centre and the North during the early Middle Ages, many towns were for a time self-governing, relatively democratic republics. Some were longer lived than others, but clearly this left a heritage of political culture very different to that of, say, Sicily, often ruled from abroad, often by a monarch whose rule was feudal, even though this had both positive and negative sides. Even during the last war, North/Centre and South had different experiences. After the signing of the Armistice in 1943, with which Italy rejected its alliance with Germany and joined the side of the Allies, the South was quickly occupied by allied forces, whilst the Centre and North lived through varying periods of hostile German occupation. The South never knew the phenomenon of a resistance movement, the North in particular did.

Geography is another factor in the North–South question. Italy is roughly one-third mountain, one-third hill, and only one-third plain. The large part of the flat land is the northern plain through which the Po flows and which stretches from Turin in the west to the Adriatic in the east. From earliest times agriculture has flourished on this plain, as much as anything because of the availability of abundant water, coming down from the surrounding mountains, particularly from the Alps to the north. Agricultural prosperity is a basis for industrial development. Flat land is also necessary for large modern factories.

In the 'leg' of Italy there are relatively few plains and much of the land is mountainous. Lalla in Unit 10 highlights the difficulty of travelling until very recent times. For much of Italian history it has been easier to do some journeys by sea rather than by road. It is also notable that over the centuries, there has been more communication from one side of the Alps to the other than across the Apennines.

Some of the mountainous terrain in the South is possible, but fairly poor, grazing land; some, notably in Calabria, offers only difficult access. The climate is hotter in the South, water is more scarce, farming more difficult. Markets are also further away. The South has considerable tourist potential, particularly on the coast, but the North and Centre also offer plentiful tourist attractions and tourism has been slower to develop in the South. Distance from centres of population, and notably from the centre of the European Union, is also a factor.

People who do not know Italy well often do not realise just how far it is from the North to the South. The maximum length is 1,200 km from Vetta d'Italia, the most northerly peak of the Italian Alps, in the Alto Adige, to Capo Isola delle Correnti, the most southerly point of Sicily. If you measure to Punta Pesce Spada, the most southerly point of Lampedusa, the most southerly of the Italian islands, it is 1,330 km. By motorway from Turin to Reggio Calabria is 1,365 km; from Milan to Reggio Calabria 1,270 km. If you wanted to go all the way to Palermo in western Sicily, add 235 km from Messina, not counting the crossing from the mainland. Motorway building started in Italy as early as the 1950s but the first one linking

Naples to the Centre and North, the Milan–Rome–Naples, l'Autostrada del Sole, was opened in the 1960s although some of the
northern sections date back to the 1950s.

All these and more are factors which mean the South has been left
behind the North and the Centre in terms of economic development
with the inevitable consequences that has for quality of life.

The economic differences between North and South constitute a
political question which has proved resistant to efforts to deal with
them. A considerable investment of public funds has been made since
the end of the Second World War to try to redress the situation, with
limited success. There are now hopeful developments in some parts
of the South but the problems which remain are huge and challenging.
On almost any measure of economic well-being, the South as a whole
falls behind the North and Centre.

Appendix 2 Dialects and minority languages

Regional accents

In Italy most people speak with an accent which indicates where they come from. Accent alone in Italy is not a marker of social class. One of the best-known local characteristics is the Florentine pronunciation of hard 'k' at the beginning of a word so that it sounds more like an 'h', giving: 'hannibale' instead of 'cannibale' (*hannibal* instead of *cannibal*) and 'hoha hola' rather than 'Coca Cola'. Further south, in Rome, single consonants may sound as though they are being doubled, whereas in Venice and the Veneto double consonants may be pronounced as if they were single. Regional differences also include vocabulary: e.g. **anguria** used in the North for water-melon – **cocomero**; and usage: e.g. in the North the **passato prossimo** is used almost exclusively as the past tense for completed actions/events, whereas in the South the **passato remoto** fulfils that function. In central Italy many people use both, switching to the **passato remoto** when in 'story-telling' mode, i.e. recounting events which are no longer relevant to their present.

Dialects

In addition many local dialects are still very much alive and for some people the preferred way to express themselves, although today it is rare to find someone who doesn't speak standard Italian as well. Italian dialects, having evolved from Latin, have much in common with each other just as Spanish and French do, and neighbouring dialects are usually mutually comprehensible. In the case of dialects geographically far apart, e.g. Venetian and Sicilian, a speaker of one is not understood by a speaker of the other. Dialects have not only a rich vocabulary, they have different verb and other grammatical forms, etc. There are vivid expressions, too, which many Italians feel are missing in standard Italian. These are the natural characteristics of a living means of communication. The national language, Italian, is a relatively recent creation as a spoken language and has not developed in the same way over centuries of daily use.

At the time of the unification of Italy (1861) it is calculated that few people, some 3 per cent, spoke Italian, which was then a literary language. For instance Vittorio Emanuele, the first king, was not at ease in Italian; he spoke Piedmontese and French. Italy having since Roman times been divided into a number of states, no national language had developed, except among a small literate and literary elite. A national language was needed for the new nation. The **questione della lingua** ('language question') was a debate at the time about how it should be created and of course taught in schools. The preferred model for some was educated Tuscan/Florentine. The existing literary language was similar to that, having evolved from the language of Petrarch and Boccaccio (both Tuscan and both fourteenth century) and other early writers, essentially because Tuscany was pre-eminent in literature at that time. But not surprisingly, progress in establishing a generalised standard language was slow. By the end of the Second World War Italian was still spoken by only about one-third of the population. Illiteracy levels were also high.

Many factors have contributed to the development of Italian. The post-war social changes spread Italian more effectively than schools. The huge internal migration (see Appendix 1) of the 1950s and 1960s meant people needed to communicate with others who did not share their dialect. Conscripts into the armed forces had for years faced this need. The growth of the mass media, notably television, has also been influential and general educational standards have improved tremendously. Nevertheless there are still people, not necessarily uneducated people, who feel they express themselves better in dialect and who use it at home and with their friends. Often they will feel that dialect words and expressions are more vivid that those of the national standard variety of Italian and import them into their speech when talking Italian. It should be noted that speaking dialect does not necessarily carry negative connotations about social status.

An enquiry conducted in December 2000 (reported on the website of ISTAT, the national statistical institute) asked 55,000 people in 20,000 families whether they used Italian, dialect or a mixture of the two in their communication with (*a*) their family, (*b*) their friends and (*c*) people they did not know. It concluded something approaching half of the sample used Italian exclusively with friends and family, and three-quarters used it with outsiders. Only 7 per cent used nothing but dialect when talking to outsiders, although 33 per cent used only dialect with their friends and the same percentage spoke dialect with their families. What was interesting was that many people, when talking to friends or to family members, mixed Italian and dialect. However the foreign learner should be able to count on Italians speaking to them in Italian.

Understanding dialects

The foreign learner should not worry too much about understanding dialects. Italians themselves do not understand dialects from other parts of Italy. People who grew up not speaking dialect at home, like Francesca (Unit 11), or from a home where dialect was not spoken because the parents were from different parts of Italy, like Sandra, will often have difficulty understanding their local dialect. Rest assured most Italians these days can also speak a fairly standard form of Italian.

Standard Italian

The foreign learner will naturally ask: what Italian should I learn? Where is the best Italian is spoken? The answer which used to be given was: in Tuscany, notably in Siena, but this was based on a rather particular idea of what Italian ought to be, rather than what in practice it was. Today most Italians use a fairly standardised form, understandable throughout the peninsula, learned at school if not at home and daily reinforced by TV and radio. Both Roman and Milanese have a strong influence on the standard model, largely because TV programmes emanate from these two cities. Model yourself on what you hear. If you absorb a regional accent, it will do no more than show where you learned your Italian.

Minority languages

Italy has a rich variety of minority languages: it is estimated some 5 per cent of the population have a mother tongue other than Italian. Linguistic minorities are specifically protected under the Constitution: 'La Repubblica tutela la lingua e la cultura delle popolazioni albanesi, catalane, germaniche, greche, slovene e croate e di quelle parlanti il francese, il francoprovenzale, il friulano, il ladino, l'occitano e il sardo' ('The Republic protects the language and culture of the

Albanian, Catalan, Germanic, Greek, Slovene and Croat [sections of the] population and of those speaking French, Francoprovençal, Friulano, Ladino, Occitan and Sardinian') (Law 482/99).

In the late 1940s Friuli-Venezia Giulia, Trentino-Alto Adige and Val d'Aosta were made autonomous regions where local languages are recognised as an acceptable means of communication for official purposes. Visitors will find road signs in Italian and either German (Alto Adige) or French (Val d'Aosta). They may find locals prefer to communicate in German or French rather than Italian, indeed they may find older people who speak Italian with difficulty. Readers might be surprised at some of the languages listed above. Here are brief notes:

Albanian (*Albanese*), spoken in an area of southern Italy and Sicily settled by Albanian refugees in the fifteenth century. The Albanian spoken is not, however, that of modern Albania, rather a form that has evolved by itself.

Catalan, in Alghero (Sardinia). The legacy of Aragonese rule of the area in the fourteenth century. As with Albanian, the Catalan spoken has developed independently of the mainland language.

Greek, spoken in isolated communities in Calabria and Puglia, a survival from the colonisation of southern Italy by the Ancient Greeks. The Greek spoken is not modern Greek and has many Italianisms.

The survival of these linguistic communities underlines just how remote and cut off from the rest of the world mountainous parts of southern Italy were until the second half of the twentieth century. In all cases, the number of speakers is diminishing.

Ladino, spoken in the various valleys in the Dolomites and Friuli – also in the Grisons canton of Switzerland.

Slovene and *Croat* are spoken on the border with Slovenia. Croatia is of course very close.

The Italian Republic through the Education Ministry encourages schools to explore their local cultural heritage and in some cases promotes the learning of local languages (Greek in Puglia, Slovene in Friuli-Venezia Giulia, for instance). The law of 1999 encourages this but what is actually done appears to be dependent on local initiatives.

Italian outside Italy

Italian is one of the four official languages of Switzerland and is spoken particularly in the Ticino Canton, which boasts an Italian-language literary tradition as well. On the east coast of Corsica, an Italian similar to Tuscan is heard, whereas in the west it is Sardinian, although the official language is French. Along the coast of Istria and Dalmatia there are Italian speakers. In addition there are Italian emigrants (some 5 million) throughout the world who retain their Italian citizenship and who cling to their Italian culture and language. Often their Italian is regional or dialectal.

A dialect poem

As an illustration of the attachment to dialect and its living nature, here is a small section of a poem in Sicilian dialect with a literal translation into Italian and a translation into English:

Un populu	Un popolo (Italian version)
mittitilu a catina,	mettetelo in catene
spugghiatilu,	spogliatelo
ttuppatici a vucca,	tappategli la bocca,
è ancora libiru.	è ancora libero.
Livatici u travagghiu,	Levategli il lavoro,
u passaportu,	il passaporto,
a tavula unni mancia,	la tavola su cui mangia,
u lettu unni dormi:	il letto in cui dorme:
è ancora riccu.	è ancora ricco.
Un populu	Un popolo
diventa povuru e servu	diventa povero e servo
quannu ci arrobannu a lingua	quando gli rubano la lingua
addutata di patri:	ricevuta dai padri:
è persu pi sempi.	è perso per sempre.

Ignazio Buttitta, poeta in dialetto siciliano, gennaio 1970

A People

put them in chains
strip them naked
seal their
voices,
they are still free.
Take away
their livelihood
their freedom to travel
the table
where they eat
the bed they sleep in,
they are still rich.
A People
become impoverished
and servile,
when the language
adopted by their fathers
is stolen:
lost forever.

Translation into English by Arthur V. Dieli

Grammar reference

Present tense (indicative) – regular verbs (see Unit 1)

Notes:

1 In listing verbs in tables we do not give the personal pronouns (**io, tu, lui,** etc.) since verbs are often used in Italian without a subject pronoun. All verbs are listed in the order: I, you (sing), he/she/it, we, you (pl), they. Note that we shall refer to verbs as being of the first group or -**are** type, etc., according to the ending of the infinitive.

2 Where the stress is irregular, the vowel in the stressed syllable is printed in italics.

1st group -are	2nd group -ere	3rd group -ire	3rd group -ire
parl**are**	scriv**ere**	fin**ire**	dorm**ire**
parl**o**	scriv**o**	fin**isco**	dorm**o**
parl**i**	scriv**i**	fin**isci**	dorm**i**
parl**a**	scriv**e**	fin**isce**	dorm**e**
parl**iamo**	scriv**iamo**	fin**iamo**	dorm**iamo**
parl**ate**	scriv**ete**	fin**ite**	dorm**ite**
parl**ano**	scr*i*v**ono**	fin*i***scono**	dorm**ono**

Note:

(*a*) Verbs like 'annegare' and 'staccare' (first conjugation, ending in -**are**) keep the same sound as in the infinitive (hard **g**, hard **c**); therefore the spelling changes when necessary to reflect this:

annego, anneghi, annega, anneghiamo, annegate, annegano (note the insertion of an **h** in front of **i** in order to keep the same sound as in the infinitive)

stacco, stacchi, stacca, stacchiamo, staccate, staccano (note the insertion of an **h** in front of **i** in order to keep the same sound as in the infinitive)

Similarly, verbs like 'lanciare', 'mangiare' and 'sbagliare' keep the same sound (soft **ch**, **j** and **ll** as in the English word **million**) and so have an **i** after **c/g/gl** unless the ending has an **i** already:

lancio, lanci, lancia, lanciamo, lanciate, lanciano; mangio, mangi, mangia, mangiamo, mangiate, mangiano; sbaglio, sbagli, sbaglia, sbagliamo, sbagliate, sbagliano

(b) Verbs like **leggere** (2nd group, ending in -ere) change the sound and therefore the spelling does not need to change:

leggo, leggi, legge, leggiamo, leggete, leggono

(c) Third group verbs (ending in -ire) are usually like 'finire': they have an -isc- inserted in the singular and in the 3rd person plural: finisco, finisci, finisce, finiamo, finite, finiscono. Verbs like 'dormire' are a fairly small group but they include some quite common verbs.

common -**ire** verbs like **finire**		common -**ire** verbs like **dormire**	
capire	proibire	aprire	soffrire
colpire	pulire	avvertire	vestire
costruire	restituire	divertire	
favorire	riferire	fuggire	
ferire	sparire	offrire	
fornire	stabilire	partire	
guarire	suggerire	scoprire	
inserire	trasferire	seguire	
obbedire	unire	sentire	
preferire		servire	

Reflexive verbs (see Unit 2)

These are conjugated as above, but the reflexive pronoun, which in the infinitive is attached at the end of the verb (e.g. vestir<u>mi</u>, vestir<u>ti</u>, vestir<u>si</u>), changes position to precede the verb in the present and other tenses.

Model: **vestirsi** (third conjugation, -ire) – to get dressed (lit. to dress oneself).

reflexive pronoun	verb	translation	lit. translation
mi	vesto	I get dressed	I dress myself
ti	vesti	you get dressed	you dress yourself
si	veste	he/she/it gets dressed	he/she/it dresses himself/herself/itself
ci	vestiamo	we get dressed	we dress ourselves
vi	vestite	you get dressed	you dress yourselves
si	vestono	they get dressed	they dress themselves

Irregular verbs – present indicative (see Unit 3)

These are the most common irregular verbs and this is a possible way of grouping them so that patterns emerge which help you to learn them.

andare	dare	fare	sapere	stare
vado	do	faccio	so	sto
vai	dai	fai	sai	stai
va	da	fa	sa	sta
andiamo	diamo	facciamo	sappiamo	stiamo
andate	date	fate	sapete	state
vanno	danno	fanno	sanno	stanno

tenere (ottenere, sostenere, appartenere)	venire (avvenire, convenire)
tengo	vengo
tieni	vieni
tiene	viene
teniamo	veniamo
tenete	venite
tengono	vengono

porre (comporre, supporre, imporre)	rimanere (permanere)	salire (assalire, trasalire)	scegliere (cogliere, sciogliere, togliere)	valere (prevalere, equivalere)
pongo	rimango	salgo	scelgo	valgo
poni	rimani	sali	scegli	vali
pone	rimane	sale	sceglie	vale
poniamo	rimaniamo	saliamo	scegliamo	valiamo
ponete	rimanete	salite	scegliete	valete
pongono	rimangono	salgono	scelgono	valgono

dovere	potere	volere
devo (debbo)	posso	voglio
devi	puoi	vuoi
deve	può	vuole
dobbiamo	possiamo	vogliamo
dovete	potete	volete
devono (debbono)	possono	vogliono

bere	sedere (possedere)	uscire (riuscire)
bevo	siedo	esco
bevi	siedi	esci
beve	siede	esce
beviamo	sediamo	usciamo
bevete	sedete	uscite
bevono	siedono	escono

dire (benedire, maledire, contraddire)	trarre (contrarre, distrarre, ritrarre)
dico	traggo
dici	trai
dice	trae
diciamo	traiamo
dite	traete
dicono	traggono

Present subjunctive – regular verbs
(see Unit 4)

Add the endings to the stem of the first person singular of the present indicative.

are	parlare	-ere, -ire	decidere	finire
-i	parli	-a	decida	finisca
-i	parli	-a	decida	finisca
-i	parli	-a	decida	finisca
-iamo	parliamo	-iamo	decidiamo	finiamo
-iate	parliate	-iate	decidiate	finiate
-ino	parlino	-ano	decidano	finiscano

Irregular present subjunctive
(see Unit 4)

Verbs which are irregular in the present indicative are also irregular in the present subjunctive. Most form the present subjunctive by adding the **2nd/3rd group endings** to the stem of the **1st person plural** of the present indicative, e.g.:

endings	essere (si-)	avere (abbi-)	fare (facci-)	dare (di-)
-a	sia	abbia	faccia	dia
-a	sia	abbia	faccia	dia
-a	sia	abbia	faccia	dia
-iamo	siamo	abbiamo	facciamo	diamo
-iate	siate	abbiate	facciate	diate
-ano	siano	abbiano	facciano	diano

Other common verbs which do this are: **bere** (**beva**), **dire** (**dica**), **piacere** (**piaccia**), **potere** (**possa**), **sapere** (**sappia**), **stare** (**stia**), **volere** (**voglia**). For some verbs, as you can see in the table below, the irregularity is similar to that of the indicative: they form the 1st and 2nd persons plural of the present subjunctive by adding the endings to the stem of the 1st person plural of the present indicative, but the other parts are similar to the present indicative.

endings	andare (vad- / and-)	uscire (esc- / usc-)	dovere (dev- / dobb-)
-a	vada	esca	deva (debba)
-a	vada	esca	deva (debba)
-a	vada	esca	deva (debba)
-iamo	andiamo	usciamo	dobbiamo
-iate	andiate	usciate	dobbiate
-ano	vadano	escano	devano (debbano)

Note:

As in the present indicative, -are verbs like 'annegare', 'staccare', 'lanciare', 'mangiare' and 'sbagliare' keep the same sound as in the infinitive, therefore change the spelling if and when necessary. Verbs ending in -ere like 'leggere' change the sound, therefore keep the same spelling as in the infinitive.

Imperfect subjunctive (see Unit 11)

Remove -re from the infinitive, and add the endings:

endings	viaggiare viaggia-	avere ave-	fornire forni-
-ssi	viaggiassi	avessi	fornissi
-ssi	viaggiassi	avessi	fornissi
-sse	viaggiasse	avesse	fornisse
-ssimo	viaggiassimo	avessimo	fornissimo
-ste	viaggiaste	aveste	forniste
-ssero	viaggiassero	avessero	fornissero

Note:

1 Verbs which have particular roots in the imperfect (e.g. **fare:** **facevo**) will have the same root in the imperfect subjunctive (**facessi** etc.).
2 **essere:** fossi, fossi, fosse, fossimo, foste, fossero
   dare: dessi, dessi, desse, dessimo, deste, dessero
   stare: stessi, stessi, stesse, stessimo, steste, stessero

Verbs and expressions followed by the subjunctive (see Unit 4 and Unit 11)

Opinion and belief	pensare che
	credere che
	avere l'impressione che
	ritenere che
	immaginare che
Doubt	aspettarsi che
	dubitare che
	non essere sicuro che
	sospettare che
Hope	augurarsi che
	desiderare che
	volere che
	sperare che
Fear	avere paura che
	temere che
Some impersonal expressions	basta che
	bisogna che
	occorrere che
	è necessario che
	è importante che

Perfect tense: *essere* or *avere*?
(see Unit 5)

The following common intransitive verbs form the perfect tense with
essere:

1   Verbs expressing movement:

andare, venire; partire, arrivare; salire, scendere; entrare, uscire

2 Verbs expressing change of state:

cambiare, crescere, diventare, nascere, morire

3 Verbs expressing state:

essere, restare, rimanere, stare

Note:

The following intransitive verbs expressing movement form the perfect tense with **avere**:

camminare, cavalcare, nuotare, passeggiare, pattinare, sciare

Irregular past participles (see Unit 5)

It can be helpful to group past participles according to their form and indeed in many of the verbs below the past participle, used as an adjective, is more used than the infinitive:

-rso	
correre – corso	perdere – perso (also: perduto)
-so	
chiudere – chiuso	tendere – teso
deludere – deluso	stendere – steso
includere – incluso	radere – raso
accendere – acceso	uccidere – ucciso
prendere – preso	decidere – deciso
scendere – sceso	ridere – riso
-sto	
rimanere – rimasto	porre – posto (and compounds, e.g.
chiedere – chiesto	comporre, esporre, riporre, deporre)
rispondere – risposto	vedere – visto (also: veduto)

-tto	
cuocere – cotto	leggere – letto
rompere – rotto	distruggere – distrutto
tradurre – tradotto	fare – fatto
dire – detto	friggere – fritto
stringere – stretto	scrivere – scritto

-sso	
discutere – discusso	smettere – smesso
mettere – messo	succedere – successo
muovere – mosso	

-nto	
fingere – finto	vincere – vinto
dipingere – dipinto	spegnere – spento

-rto	
aprire – aperto	morire – morto
coprire – coperto	

Note also:

essere – stato; bere – bevuto (from **bevere** – an older form of the verb); **nascere – nato; vivere – vissuto; venire – venuto.**

Conditional and future
(see Unit 8 and Unit 9)

1. For verbs in the 2nd and 3rd group, add the endings to the infinitive without the final -e, e.g. **scrivere: scriver-**.

2. For verbs in the 1st group (-**are** verbs), add the endings to the infinitive without the final -e but with the -a- becoming -e-, e.g. **parlare: parler-**.

Conditional (see Unit 8)

endings	parlare	scrivere	finire	dormire
-ei	parlerei	scriverei	finirei	dormirei
-esti	parleresti	scriveresti	finiresti	domiresti
-ebbe	parlerebbe	scriverebbe	finirebbe	dormirebbe
-emmo	parleremmo	scriveremmo	finiremmo	dormiremmo
-este	parlereste	scrivereste	finireste	dormireste
-ebbero	parlerebbero	scriverebbero	finirebbero	dormirebbero

Future (see Unit 9)

endings	parlare	scrivere	finire	dormire
-ò	parlerò	scriverò	finirò	dormirò
-ai	parlerai	scriverai	finirai	domirai
-à	parlerà	scriverà	finirà	dormirà
-emo	parleremo	scriveremo	finiremo	dormiremo
-ete	parlerete	scriverete	finirete	dormirete
-anno	parleranno	scriveranno	finiranno	dormiranno

Irregular conditional (see Unit 7 and Unit 8) and future (see Unit 9)

Note:

Verbs which are irregular in the conditional are irregular in the future. They are:

1 Verbs (and their compounds) where the infinitive ending has dropped the first -a- or -e- as well as the second and has become shortened to -r-:

andare – andrei – andrò; avere – avrei – avrò; cadere – cadrei – cadrò; dovere – dovrei – dovrò; godere – godrei – godrò; parere – parrei – parrò; potere – potrei – potrò; sapere – saprei – saprò; vedere – vedrei – vedrò; vivere – vivrei – vivrò

2 Verbs (and their compounds) where the stem ends in -l- or -n-: in these the l/n are replaced by r, giving a double r:

dolere – dorrei – dorrò; rimanere – rimmarrei – rimarrò; tenere – terrei – terrò; valere – varrei – varrò; venire – verrei – verrò; volere – vorrei – vorrò

3 Note also:

bere (from old Italian bevere) – berrei – berrò; essere – sarei – sarò; dare – darei – darò; stare – starei – starò

Imperative (see Unit 8)

	parlare	scrivere	finire	dormire
sing – **tu** form	parla!	scrivi!	finisci!	dormi!
sing – **Lei** form	parli!	scriva!	finisca!	dorma!
1st plur	parliamo!	scriviamo!	finiamo!	dormiamo!
2nd plur	parlate!	scrivete!	finite!	dormite!

Negative imperative – *tu* form
(see Unit 8)

parlare	scrivere	finire	dormire
non parlare!	non scrivere!	non finire!	non dormire!

Irregular imperative (see Unit 8)

Most verbs that are irregular in the present are also irregular in the informal imperative and follow the same pattern, e.g.: **tenere – tieni!**; **venire – vieni!**

However, note also:

	sing – 'tu' form	1st plur	2nd plur
andare	vai! / va'!	andiamo!	andate!
avere	abbi!	abbiamo!	abbiate!
dare	dai! / da'!	diamo!	date!
dire	di'!	diciamo!	dite!
essere	sii!	siamo!	siate!
fare	fai! / fa'!	facciamo!	fate!
stare	stai! / sta'!	stiamo!	state!

Imperfect (see Unit 10)

Remove -**re** from the infinitive and add the endings, which are the same for each of the three types of verb:

endings	viagg**iare**	av**ere**	forn**ire**
-**vo**	viaggia**vo**	ave**vo**	forni**vo**
-**vi**	viaggia**vi**	ave**vi**	forni**vi**
-**va**	viaggia**va**	ave**va**	forni**va**
-**vamo**	viaggia**vamo**	ave**vamo**	forni**vamo**
-**vate**	viaggia**vate**	ave**vate**	forni**vate**
-**vano**	viaggia**vano**	ave**vano**	forn**ivano**

Irregular imperfect (see Unit 10)

1 **essere**: ero, eri, era, eravamo, eravate, *e*rano

2 Verbs with infinitives which are contractions of earlier, longer ones: the root is the longer form. The endings, however, are regular:

> **dire** (from **dicere** = **dice-**): dicevo, dicevi, diceva, dicevamo, dicevate, dic*e*vano

> **fare** (from **facere** = **face-**): facevo, facevi, etc.

> **bere** (from **bevere** = **beve-**): bevevo, bevevi, etc.

> **produrre** (from **producere** = **produce-**): producevo, producevi, etc. (and all verbs ending in **-durre**, e.g. **condurre, sedurre**)

> **porre** (from **ponere** = **pone-**): ponevo, ponevi, etc. (and all compounds of **porre**, e.g. **proporre, riporre**)

Past definite (see Unit 12)

Add the endings to the verb stem.

-are verbs		**-ere** verbs		**-ire** verbs	
endings	parl**are**	endings	vend**ere**	endings	forn**ire**
-ai	parl**ai**	**-ei (-etti)**	vend**ei** (vend**etti**)	**-ii**	forn**ii**
-sti	parl**asti**	**-esti**	vend**esti**	**-isti**	forn**isti**
-ò	parl**ò**	**-ette**	vend**ette**	**-ì**	forn**ì**
-ammo	parl**ammo**	**-emmo**	vend**emmo**	**-immo**	forn**immo**
-aste	parl**aste**	**-este**	vend**este**	**-iste**	forn**iste**
-arono	parl**arono**	**-erono** (**-ettero**)	vend**erono** (vend**ettero**)	**-irono**	forn**i**rono

Irregular past definite (see Unit 12)

Note:

The 1st and 3rd person singular and the 3rd person plural follow one pattern; the 2nd person singular and the 1st and 2nd person plural a different one.

avere	ebbi, avesti, ebbe, avemmo, aveste, ebbero
essere	fui, fosti, fu, fummo, foste, furono
bere	bevvi, bevesti, bevve, bevemmo, beveste, bevvero
chiedere	chiesi, chiedesti, chiese, chiedemmo, chiedeste, chiesero
chiudere	chiusi, chiudesti, chiuse, chiudemmo, chiudeste, chiusero
conoscere	conobbi, conoscesti, conobbe, conoscemmo, conosceste, conobbero
correre	corsi, corresti, corse, corremmo, correste, corsero
dare	diedi (detti), desti, diede (dette), demmo, deste, diedero (dettero)
decidere	decisi, decidesti, decise, decidemmo, decideste, decisero
dire	dissi, dicesti, disse, dicemmo, diceste, dissero
fare	feci, facesti, fece, facemmo, faceste, fecero
leggere	lessi, leggesti, lesse, leggemmo, leggeste, lessero
mettere	misi, mettesti, mise, mettemmo, metteste, misero
nascere	nacqui, nascesti, nacque, nascemmo, nasceste, nacquero
perdere	persi, perdesti, perse, perdemmo, perdeste, persero
prendere	presi, prendesti, prese, prendemmo, prendeste, presero
rimanere	rimasi, rimanesti, rimase, rimanemmo, rimaneste, rimasero
rispondere	risposi, rispondesti, rispose, rispondemmo, rispondeste, risposero
sapere	seppi, sapesti, seppe, sapemmo, sapeste, seppero
scegliere	scelsi, scegliesti, scelse, scegliemmo, sceglieste, scelsero
scendere	scesi, scendesti, scese, scendemmo, scendeste, scesero
scrivere	scrissi, scrivesti, scrisse, scrivemmo, scriveste, scrissero
stare	stetti, stesti, stette, stemmo, steste, stettero
vedere	vidi, vedesti, vide, vedemmo, vedeste, videro
venire	venni, venisti, venne, venimmo, veniste, vennero
vivere	vissi, vivesti, visse, vivemmo, viveste, vissero
volere	volli, volesti, volle, volemmo, voleste, vollero

Verbs followed by the infinitive, *di* + infinitive and *a* + infinitive (see Unit 6)

Verbs followed by the infinitive

amare	piacere
desiderare	preferire
detestare	sapere
dovere	potere
odiare	volere
osare	

Expressions followed by infinitive

bisogna	è necessario
è importante	è opportuno
è interessante	è possibile

Verbs followed by a + *infinitive*

abituarsi a	iniziare a
aiutare a	insegnare a
cominciare a	mettersi a
continuare a	provare a
divertirsi a	rinunciare a
imparare a	riuscire a

Verbs followed by di + *infinitive*

accettare di	ricordarsi di
accorgersi di	rifiutare di
ammettere di	rischiare di
avere bisogno/intenzione/	sforzarsi di
paura/vergogna/voglia di	smettere di
cercare di	sognare di
chiedere di	sperare di
decidere di	stufarsi di
dimenticarsi di	temere di
fare finta di	tentare di
finire di	vantarsi di
minacciare di	non vedere l'ora di
pretendere di	vergognarsi di
rendersi conto di	

Verbs followed by **a** + *the person you are addressing and* **di** + *infinitive*

dire a qualcuno di	proibire a qualcuno di
domandare a qualcuno di	promettere a qualcuno di
impedire a qualcuno di	proporre a qualcuno di
ordinare a qualcuno di	vietare a qualcuno di
permettere a qualcuno di	

Personal pronouns

See Unit 2 for subject pronouns; Unit 3 for object pronouns; Unit 4 for combined pronouns; Unit 5 for agreement with past participle; Unit 6 for position with gerund; Unit 7 for position with **volere, dovere, potere.**

	subject	direct object		indirect object	
		stressed	unstressed	stressed	unstressed
1st sing	io	me	mi	(a) me	mi
2nd sing	tu	te	ti	(a) te	ti
3rd sing masc	lui	lui	lo	(a) lui	gli
3rd sing fem	lei	lei	la	(a) lei	le
polite form	Lei	Lei	La	(a) Lei	Le
1st plur	noi	noi	ci	(a) noi	ci
2nd plur	voi	voi	vi	(a) voi	vi
3rd plur masc	loro	loro	li	(a) loro	gli
3rd plur fem	loro	loro	le	(a) loro	gli

Question words (see Unit 4)

Quando? When?
Dove? Where?
Come? How?
Perché? Why?
Quanto? Quanti? How much? How many?
Chi? Who?
Che cosa? *often:* **Cosa?** *sometimes:* **Che?** What?

Quale? (Qual? *in front of* è, era – *no apostrophe*) Quali? Which one?
What? (*meaning* What sort of?) Which ones?

Note:

Che is used in two ways:

1 Meaning 'what': Che fai? This can also be: Che cosa fai? Cosa
   fai? Che fai would be the most careful, formal language, cosa fai
   the most colloquial.
2 Meaning 'what sort of', indeed sometimes the question is: Che
   tipo di . . . ? Che vita fai? 'What sort of life do you lead?'

Che and quale with essere

(*a*) che (che cosa, cosa) is used when the expected answer is a definition, e.g. Che cos'è il panettone? 'What is panettone?' Il panettone
è il dolce tradizionale di Natale in Italia. 'It is the traditional
Christmas cake in Italy.'

(*b*) quale is used when the expected answer is an identification, given
a choice of:

1 either one of two options: e.g. Qual è il tuo dolce natalizio
   preferito, il panettone o il pandoro? 'Which is your favourite
   Christmas cake, panettone or pandoro?' Il mio dolce preferito è
   il panettone. 'My favourite Christmas cake is panettone.'
2 or one option from an abstract set: e.g. Qual è il dolce tradizionale
   di Natale in Italia? 'What is the traditional Christmas cake in
   Italy?' E' il panettone. 'It is panettone.' (Panettone being one cake
   among all Italian cakes.)

Therefore, in Italian, you ask: Qual è il tuo numero di telefono?
'What is your telephone number?' and *not*: Che cos'è il tuo numero
di telefono? to which the reply would be a definition ('My telephone
number is a seven-digit code that you have to dial if you want to
contact me by phone').

And equally: Qual è il tuo indirizzo? 'What is your address?' Qual
è il tuo lavoro? 'What is your job?'

Key to exercises

Unit 1

Exercise 1

1 Francesca Tonzig. Her family name sounds Slavonic/Russian. Francesca says it is of a type not uncommon in the area near the frontier with Slovenia. **2** Teresa. She speaks English, French and Greek. **3** Francesca. At the time of the interview, she had been living in England for six months.

Exercise 2

1 è/si chiama; È; vive/risiede; studia; fa; conosce/studia; Vive. **2** ha; viene/è; sono; suonano/sembrano; finiscono; finisce.

Exercise 3

Check your answers in the verb table in the Grammar reference.

Exercise 4

1 Teresa, da quanto vivi a Norwich? Vivo a Norwich da cinque o sei anni.
2 Teresa, da quanto tempo fai il dottorato? Faccio il dottorato da tre anni.
3 Francesca, da quando studi il francese? Studio il francese da Natale.
4 Francesca, da quanto tempo lavori come interprete? Lavoro come interprete da sei mesi.

Exercise 5

1 His father, a farmer, encouraged him to seek a life which was not so hard.
2 Because his business had grown. **3** Just one, at 10 via San Tommaso in the centre of Turin. **4** It made it possible to conserve the aroma of the roasted coffee. **5** The company started to build new premises on the outskirts of Turin.
6 Because coffee imports were banned. **7** He set up a centre for research into coffee. **8** It was chosen as the supplier of coffee for the World Cup (soccer). It was 103 years old.

Exercise 6

1 Nel milleottocentoottantacinque. **2** Nel milleottocentonovantaquattro.
3 Il milleottocentonovantacinque. **4** Nel millenovecentodieci. **5** Dal
millenovecentotrentanove al millenovecentoquarantacinque. **6** Dal
millenovecentosettantuno. **7** Il millenovecentoottantotto.

Unit 2

Exercise 1

1 Lalla, whose real name is Maria Rossi. **2** Marco, who lives in Caprie, near
Avigliana, a small town in Piedmont. **3** Marco and Bea. They live in Caprie.
4 Angelo Corica.

Exercise 2

1 Io; Io; Lui. **2** Io; (no pronoun); io; lei. **3** Io; tu; Io;
(no prounoun); Tu; Io. **4** Lei; io; Lei. Io; (no pronoun).

Note: Don't forget there is no hard and fast rule; whether to use a pronoun or
not is a question of emphasis.

Exercise 3

1 Io mi chiamo Giovanna, sono sposata, ho 55 anni, sono casalinga e sono
nata a Bari. Le presento (questa è) mia sorella, Paola. Lei è avvocato, è single
(non è sposata), ha 45 anni, è nata a Napoli. **2** Io sono/mi chiamo Enrico. Ho
21 anni, sono studente di medicina, e vivo e risiedo in Italia; questo è mio
fratello, Marco. Ha 26 anni, è giornalista ed è residente in Inghilterra.

Exercise 4

1 He works in Milan. **2** He wakes at 7. He watches TV in the morning, the TV
news bulletins, the Maurizio Costanzo Show and then gets breakfast in a bar, as
Italians often do, and goes to the office where he starts by reading the papers.
He doesn't give details of how he works but says the script for the programme
is ready by about 7 pm although sometimes things are changed even as the
programme goes out. He points out although the programme appears
improvised it is carefully prepared. **3** He says he doesn't read them carefully and
he skips the sport which doesn't interest him. **4** His home is in Alassio. He
obviously enjoys it: he talks about the clean air, the sea, friends. **5** He enjoys
having money and spending but he has his feet on the ground, he knows his
luck could change. **6** Nothing is worse than explaining jokes! However: Ricci

plays on the word 'autore' – by saying yes, he is an author, after all one can be the author (perpetrator) of a robbery. He describes the daylight coming in through curtains which don't meet properly as a 'technical reason' for waking up early. He talks about melatonin and jet-lag when all he means is he went to bed very late. And saying that needing anything more to eat than a tomato is 'prostitution' is just a jokey way of saying he is quite capable of living simply.

Exercise 5

a. si alza; si lava; si veste; si fa; si toglie; si sveste; si fa; si mette; si corica; si addormenta. **b.** mi alzo; mi lavo; mi vesto; mi faccio; mi tolgo; mi svesto; mi faccio; mi metto; mi corico; mi addormento.

Note: Some of these verbs, e.g. fare, togliere, are irregular. See Unit 3.

Exercise 6

1 si annoiano g. **2** si divertono f. **3** si arrabbia d. **4** ci rallegriamo e.
5 mi innervosisco c. **6** si entusiasma a. **7** ti stupisci b.

Unit 3

Exercise 1

1 She has one brother – and two sisters (*un maschio e due femmine*, but all three are *fratelli*). **2** They each have a large nose. **3** She has fleshy lips, a straight nose, big black eyes and shiny black hair.

Exercise 2

The answers are in the text.

Exercise 3

Siena: C'è; c'è; ci sono; c'è; c'è; c'è; ci vuole; c'è; C'è.
Padova: c'è; c'è; ci sono; c'è; ci sono; Ci sono; ci sono.

Exercise 4

occhi, occhioni, occhietti, occhiacci

mani, manone, manine, manacce (*manone* because *mano* is feminine, *-one* added to feminine nouns becomes *-ona*, plural *-one*)

denti, dentoni, dentini

piedi, piedoni, piedini

Exercise 5

1 False. **2** False (she says she hates it, it is a problem when buying clothes, but in paragraph 3 you may think she is rather proud of her figure). **3** True. **4** False (she says she is 'insignificant, stupid')

Exercise 6

1 aggraziato/sgraziato, goffo; alto/basso; asciutto/in carne; atletico, in forma/fuori forma; attraente, sexy, bello/brutto; effeminato/mascolino; grasso/magro; imponente, muscoloso, robusto/mingherlino; slanciato, snello, sottile/tarchiato. **2** Up to you!

Exercise 7

Some verbs occur more than once. You probably found: **1** ho 17 anni. **2** le mie idee sono. **3** Ho un sacco. **4** ma so ascoltare. **5** Ho un bel viso. **6** che è un gran problema. **7** è incredibilmente difficile. **8** Veniamo a lui. **9** il paragone è. **10** lui ha la fidanzata. **11** lo dicono tutti. **12** Sono infelice. **13** La sua attuale ragazza è bassa. **14** sai?

Unit 4

Exercise 1

1 He says she walks purposefully, as if towards a goal. **2** She is constantly on the move, running here and there, whether around the town or at home. **3** Openness and a willingness to help people, to listen to them and have a dialogue with them.

Exercise 2

1 Ne ho tre. **2** Ne ho tredici. **3** Ne ho quindici. **4** Ne ho sette. **5** Ne ho cinquantatré. **6** Ne ho ventitré.

Exercise 3

Marta spera che Gianni
1 non *ami* il calcio. **2** non *sia* vegetariano. **3** *sia* appassionato di musica latino-americana e *sappia* suonare la chitarra.

Gianni *spera* che Marta
4 *sia* bruna. **5** *abbia* la voce dolce. **6** *ami* viaggiare. **8** *adori* i ristoranti di pesce.

Exercise 4

1 *Penso che* mio padre *sia* una persona disponibile. **2** *Penso che* mia madre *dia* molta importanza alla famiglia. **3** *Penso che* i miei fratelli *lavorino* troppo. **4** *Penso di avere* un atteggiamento positivo verso la vita. **5** *Penso che* i miei nonni *siano* affettuosi. **6** *Penso di essere* una persona intraprendente.

Exercise 5

1 *-oso* = *-ous* (full of): *avventuroso* – adventurous; *coraggioso* – courageous; *nervoso* – nervous; *pauroso* – fearful (*paura* = fear); *presuntuoso* – presumptuous (although meaning 'proud, arrogant', rather than 'bold, forward'). Sometimes we find the meaning but then have to find the right English word: *noioso* – boring (*noia* – boredom); *spiritoso* – witty (that is full of *spirito* – wit). **2** *-abile/ibile* = *-ble* (able to be): *affidabile* – reliable; *inaffidabile* – unreliable; *flessibile* – flexible; *inflessibile* – inflexible; *suscettibile* – susceptible (also 'touchy', 'easily offended'). **3** *testone* (stubborn), from *testa* (head). Perhaps also: *spendaccione* (see **5**). **4** *-ista*. Note the *-a* ending, same for masculine and feminine. The reason for the *-a* ending in the masculine singular lies in the history of Italian language. **5** *solare* (with a sunny disposition), from *sole* (sun); *spendaccione* (a big spender, spendthrift) from *spendere* (to spend money).

Exercise 6

Her mother: Penso che mia madre sia una mamma severa. Lei invece non è d'accordo con me, e pensa di essere una persona flessibile. Io credo anche che mia mamma sia una persona molto attiva, una lavoratrice. Lei invece ritiene di essere piuttosto pigra.

Her brother: Penso che mio fratello sia un uomo piuttosto attraente, mi sembra che sia sexy. Lui invece crede di essere abbastanza brutto, però pensa di essere una persona piuttosto avventurosa, mentre io ritengo che sia un po' troppo prudente.

Her sister: Credo che mia sorella sia estroversa e socievole, ma lei pensa di essere timida. Io penso anche che lei sia una persona egoista, mentre lei crede di essere generosa e affettuosa.

Exercise 7

Answers	A	B	C	D	E	F
Questions	4	1	5	2	3	6

Exercise 8

1 Come si chiamano? **2** Di dove sono / vengono? **3** Che lingua parlano? **4** Da quanto tempo vivono lì? **5** Che lavoro fanno? **6** Quanti anni hanno? **7** Quanti figli hanno? **8** Quanti anni hanno i loro figli? **9** Quanti cani hanno? **10** Perché passano sempre la notte svegli / in piedi? **11** Chi gli telefona ogni notte alle 3? **12** Perché rispondono al telefono e poi cominciano a passare l'aspirapolvere?

Unit 5

Exercise 1

1 The relationship began in a most romantic way at a masked ball, where Angelo invited Lalla to dance a waltz. But at the time, 1958, in the North, where Lalla came from and where they met, Southerners were regarded with suspicion and often antipathy so the couple faced attitudes that were effectively racist.
2 She says she enjoys a challenge, hates prejudice and thinks that diversity is a stimulus and that those who are prepared to try can bring out positive things from it.

Exercise 2

1 ha invitato. **2** si sono conosciuti. **3** si sono innamorati. **4** hanno deciso.
5 sono (sempre) piaciute.

Exercise 3

parlato, saputo, spedito, trovato, dovuto, uscito,
aspettato, tenuto, dormito, cantato, voluto, finito

Exercise 4

2 Si è vestita; si è truccata; si è pettinata. **3** Ha chiamato. **4** è arrivato; è salita; ha dato. **5** ha pagato; è uscita. **6** È entrata. **7** si sono incontrati; ha invitato.
8 hanno ballato. **9** è finito; hanno cominciato. **10** ha domandato.

Exercise 5

1 Because it was her twentieth birthday. **2** She usually arrived late for class. And because she was late that day, her usual place was taken so that she had to sit at the back – which happened to be near Marco. **3** No. For some time they were just friends. It was some seven years later that things changed. **4** The change from friendship to something more came about because they saw more of each other playing bridge.

Exercise 6

sono andata a sedermi in fondo
gli ho detto di farmi gli auguri per il mio compleanno
se n'è accorto
mi ha fatto gli auguri
siamo rimasti amici
abbiamo cominciato a frequentarci
è scoccata la scintilla
ci siamo sposati

Exercise 7

1 transitive (Ho corso <u>la maratona</u>); intransitive. **2** intransitive; transitive (Ho sceso <u>le scale</u>). **3** transitive (Ho migliorato <u>il record del mondo</u>); intransitive. **4** transitive (Ho peggiorato <u>la situazione</u>); intransitive. **5** intransitive; transitive (Ho saltato <u>due giorni di scuola</u>). **6** transitive (Ho finito <u>di studiare</u> alle otto); intransitive. **7** intransitive; transitive (Ho cominciato <u>a lavorare</u> nel 1998).

Exercise 8

2 *Sono uscito* con Francesca *per* 3 mesi = I dated Francesca for 3 months (we are not dating each other any more). *Esco* con Francesca *da* 3 mesi = I have been dating Francesca for 3 months (we are still dating each other). **3** *Sono stato* a dieta *per* 10 giorni = I was on a diet for 10 days (I am not any more). *Sono* a dieta *da* 10 giorni = I have been on a diet for 10 days (I still am). **4** *Sono vissuto* in Canada *per* 40 anni = I lived in Canada for 40 years (I don't live there any more). *Vivo* in Canada *da* 40 anni = I have been living in Canada for 40 years (I still live there). **5** *Ho frequentato* un corso di yoga *per* 5 settimane = I did yoga (went to a yoga class) for 5 weeks (I am not doing it any more). *Frequento* un corso di yoga *da* 5 settimane = I have being doing yoga for 5 weeks (I still am). **6** *Ho cantato* in un coro *per* 6 mesi = I sang in a choir for 6 months (I am not singing any more). *Canto* in un coro *da* 6 mesi = I have been singing in a choir for 6 months (I still am). **7** *Ho lavorato* in banca *per* 15 anni = I worked in a bank for 15 years (I am not working in a bank any more). *Lavoro* in banca *da* 15 anni = I have been working in a bank for 15 years (I still am).

Exercise 9

Maria – Aldo; Luisa – Maurizio; Franca – Umberto; Eleonora – Francesco.

Unit 6

Exercise 1

1 He hoped to make a university career in Bologna. In the end he became a family doctor in Turin. **2** It was clear that the professor who had promised him advancement was not going to keep his promise, Angelo's father had died and his financial situation meant he needed to earn his living another way.

Exercise 2

deciso, risposto, messo, stato, scritto, vissuto

If you did not know any of these, don't worry. Consult the Grammar reference now.

Exercise 3

1 Mi sono iscritto all'Università di Roma nel 1952. **2** Ho studiato ingegneria per 5 anni. **3** Mi sono laureato in ingegneria civile nel 1957. **4** Sono rimasto a Roma per un anno ed ho lavorato per il Comune. **5** Ho fatto il servizio militare in Sicilia. **6** Nel 1959, ho scelto di vivere in una piccola città a Nord di Roma, Grosseto, ed ho aperto uno studio privato con un collega. **7** Ho lavorato in proprio per 40 anni. **8** Ho scritto per molte riviste specializzate ed ho vinto alcuni appalti importanti. **9** Sono andato in pensione nel 1999. **10** Sono in pensione da 3 anni.

Exercise 4

1 Her family was going through a bad patch financially and, with her sisters, she went out to work. She tried to keep up her studies but she didn't have sufficient determination and she preferred working. She enjoyed being financially indopondont. **2** Sho montions working for the European Community in Brussels, where she enjoyed being a young single woman. She says she enjoyed travelling. But when she had children, she stopped working to look after them and she says that she enjoyed that greatly and found it perhaps the most stimulating of all her jobs. **3** She trained as a Family Counsellor and worked in a voluntary capacity helping families. She obviously found it deeply satisfying to work on all areas of family life.

Exercise 5

Other examples could be:

Nel 1950 *ho smesso di* studiare.
Nel 1957 *ho dovuto* trasferirmi in Francia per motivi di famiglia.
Nel 1961 *ho iniziato a* lavorare per una compagnia di assicurazioni.
Nel 1977 ho avuto un figlio, ma *ho continuato a* lavorare a tempo pieno.
Nel 1988 *ho finito di* scrivere il mio libro.
Nel 1965 *ho voluto* cambiare lavoro.
Nel 2001 *ho tentato di* finire gli studi universitari.
Nel 1990 *ho cercato di* prendere il diploma di infermiere professionale.
Nel 1942 *ho provato a* studiare il giapponese.
Nel 1972 *ho potuto* comprare una casa al mare.
Nel 1999 *ho deciso di* andare a vivere in Italia.
Nel 1983 *ho scelto di* andare in pensione con cinque anni di anticipo.

Exercise 6

1 One from Malaysia and one from Argentina. **2** They are his adoptive parents. **3** His natural mother. **4** He found friends he liked and who were helpful, and he also found the officers very 'human' – he probably means they were understanding and treated him well. **5** He seems to have been touched that these women who are are very much on the margins of society should applaud him, in his uniform which showed him to be a representative of the law, because of their shared skin colour.

Exercise 7

The answers to this must inevitably be personal to you.

Unit 7

Exercise 1

1 False – it is 1.75 per cent (the text said 17.5 per thousand). **2** True. The North-East is a 'boom area' with thriving economic activity and a shortage of labour, a natural magnet for incoming workers. **3** False. It has tripled. **4** True. **5** True: 50 per 1,000. **6** True. **7** False. It has stayed the same, but because of a rising number of immigrants and not an increase in births.

Exercise 2

The stages the new EC recruits must go through are:

1 They come to Italy at least a couple of months before they are due to start work. Armed with a short contract from the school, they go to the main Police Station and apply for a work permit. **2** They then go back to the country where they are working and finish their job there, working out their term of notice. **3** They come back to Italy. At some point, possibly during the initial visit, they will also have found somewhere to live while working in the school. They collect their work permit and apply for residence in Italy. (They must apply to the *Comune* where they live for this, and get a *certificato di residenza*.) This process takes about three weeks. In practice they often start work. **4** Once they have a certificate saying they are resident they can apply for a *libretto di lavoro*. (This is done at the *Ufficio di Collocamento*.) And once they have that the employer can officially take them on as employees. Residence has to be at a specific address and technically the authorities are supposed to check that the person is in fact living there.

Note: Not all this information was in the text but we hope it may perhaps be useful. Remember, however, that procedures etc. are subject to modification.

Exercise 3

1 puoi cercare. **2** devi mandare. **3** devi aspettare. **4** devi venire. **5** devono dare.
6 devi andare. **7** devi richiedere. **8** può fare. **9** puoi lasciare. **10** dovete andare.
11 dovete richiedere. **12** può ottenere. **13** puoi firmare. **14** possono impiegare.
15 devi cominciare. **16** devo spedire.

Exercise 4

1 Martedì pomeriggio *vorrei andare* in piscina per fare un po' di esercizio, ma
dovrei essere presente alla riunione settimanale con il direttore. *Potrei andare* in
piscina all'ora di pranzo. **2** Mercoledì mattina *vorrei fare* un po' di spesa, ma
dovrei lavorare in ufficio dalle 9 alle 5. Forse *potrei entrare* alle 10 e *lavorare*
fino alle 6. **3** Giovedì pomeriggio *vorrei fare* i compiti per il corso di italiano, ma
dovrei anche *andare* a Milano per un appuntamento. *Potrei andare* a Milano in
treno, e *fare* i compiti durante il viaggio. **4** Venerdì pomeriggio *vorrei uscire*
presto dal lavoro per passare il fine settimana in montagna, ma *dovrei* anche
incontrare un cliente importante. *Potrei spostare* l'appuntamento con il cliente
alla mattina.

Exercise 5

1 Mi dispiace! Non *ho potuto prenotare* la vacanza al mare perché *sono
dovuto/a andare* dal parrucchiere. **2** Mi dispiace! Non *ho potuto depositare*
l'assegno in banca perché *ho dovuto lavorare* fino a tardi. **3** Mi dispiace!
Non *ho potuto fare* i compiti di italiano perché *ho dovuto accompagnare* mia
figlia a una festa. **4** Mi dispiace! Non *ho potuto fare* la spesa perché *sono
dovuta andare* dal dentista.

Exercise 6

1 The quotas for non-EU employees, and the uncertainty of the outcome of an
application to employ one, mean that the school might find itself without the
necessary teacher at the start of the school year. In the same way the
prospective teacher might find he/she cannot get permission to work in Italy
and therefore has no job for the following year. It is therefore safer for the
school and fairer to prospective employees to employ EC nationals.
2 Executives, managers have favourable treatment. Multinational companies
often bring non-EU employees into their Italian branches in management
capacities.

Unit 8

Exercise 1

1 True. **2** True. **3** False, the manager is required for a new shop opening in Turin. **4** False, they must be under 35. **5** False, a high school diploma is the basic academic requirement. **6** True. **7** False. **8** True.

Exercise 2

(a) *conoscitore* to know: connoisseur, expert; *venditrice*: to sell – seller, sales assistant (female); *gestore*: to manage – manager; *scrittore*: to write – writer; *lettrice*: to read – reader (female).

(b) *conoscenza*: to know – knowledge, also: a person known, acquaintance; *provenienza*: to originate, to come from – origin; *gestione*: to manage – management; *maturazione*: to ripen, mature – ripening, ripeness; *vendita*: to sell, sale; *crescita*: to grow – growth.

(c) Note: as well as your likely guess, we give you an Italian dictionary definition and a one word translation. **1** Your likely guess: *una persona che ristora*. Lo Zingarelli: 1 *Gestore di ristorante* (restaurateur); 2 *Rimedio, medicina che ristora* (tonic). **2** Your likely guess: *una persona che assicura*. Lo Zingarelli: 1 *Ente che assume il rischio oggetto del contratto di assicurazione* (insurer – in the sense of the company); 2 (f. *-trice*) *Correntemente, chi stipula contratti di assicurazione come agente di una società assicuratrice* (insurer – the person who draws up the contract of insurance). **3** Your likely guess: *una persona che mette liquido in bottiglie*. Lo Zingarelli: 1 (f. *-trice*) *Chi imbottiglia vino o liquori per mestiere* (person whose job is to bottle wine or liquor); 2 *Apparecchio per riempire le bottiglie* (machine, plant for bottling).

Exercise 3

1 She works with the organization of the London dress shows for Krizia and Missoni; she interprets for the London office of the Centro Fiorentino Pitti, and as a translator, mainly for Vogue on-line Magazine, translating it into Italian. **2** Because it has enabled her to learn more about the international fashion world and she is proud to be promoting the Italian collections abroad. **3** Because she wants to move to Milan, with her husband whom she has recently married. She also wants to give up the dress show work so as to have more time to herself.

Exercise 4

1 lavorerebbe; cercherebbe; **2** preferirebbe; **3** manderebbe.

Exercise 5

1 Sbucci; affetti. **2** Lavi. **3** Sbollenti; sbucci. **4** Metta. **5** Aggiunga. **6** Faccia. **7** tolga; lasci. **8** passi.

Exercise 6

1 <u>Non usare</u> la toilette nelle stazioni! **2** <u>Non sporgerti</u> dal finestrino! **3** <u>Non tirare</u> il freno di emergenza! **4** <u>Non mettere</u> i piedi sui sedili!

Exercise 7

1 Not only knowledge of the English language but familiarity with English and American ways of life and of thinking. Also willingness to travel regularly between Italy and UK / North America. **2** She has lived in London for 20 years and often travelled to New York, where she also lived for a couple of years. Moreover her mother was born in Bristol and so she grew up in contact with English ways of thinking.

Exercise 8

1 Cerco qualcuno che <u>sia</u> diplomato. **2** Cerco qualcuno che <u>abbia</u> esperienza di lavoro nel settore. **3** Cerco qualcuno che <u>sappia</u> usare: MS Word, Excel, Access. **4** Cerco qualcuno che <u>sia</u> disponibile a fare straordinari se necessario.

Unit 9

Exercise 1

1 The number of family units in Italy is rising but the population is not. **2** 'Famiglia mononucleare'. **3** 1.25 children per couple (i.e. using a decimal point, not a comma). **4** She refers to a dramatic rise in separations and divorces and, further on, to an 'avalanche' of divorced and separated persons. **5** There are those who choose to remain unmarried; there are the divorced and separated (the writer uses a phrase: 'single di ritorno', those who go back to being single); and there are the elderly, mostly women, many widows, who often live alone.

Exercise 2

1 No, she had one brother. **2** Father went out to work and mother stayed at home, looking after the children and the home. **3** She will want to continue working so she will not be at home for them as her mother was for her and her brother. **4** They are economic: they put off having children until they are financially secure since they feel obliged to supply things such as a computer, toys etc. which children nowadays want.

Note: The last passage of this unit on the costs of parenthood.

Exercise 3

1 fa/sta facendo. **2** va. **3** lavora/sta lavorando. **4** va. **5** ama. compra.

Exercise 4

2d; 3f; 4b; 5c; 6a.

Exercise 5

1 They want to put to use what they have studied, if they have studied. She does not mention that many women work because they want a higher standard of living than is possible on the earnings of one person (cf. what Teresa said about the cost of bringing up a child today, with its sophisticated wants) – that is certainly a factor. And of course there are single mothers. **2** Family life is fragmented. The family does not spend much time together as a unit in the way they used to. **3** The speed with which it has taken place. **4** The fact that the government does nothing to help families with the care of children.

Exercise 6

The examples she gives are:

1 Parents support children through university which very few finish in the time specified and many never finish. *Note:* There is indeed a high drop-out rate; in an attempt to counter this a new short degree (*laurea breve*) has been introduced. **2** Parents support children while they look for a proper, permanent job. This may mean supporting them while they do a masters degree, which often means the 'child' going abroad to study. **3** Parents help children set up home and help them with the costs of bringing up their children if/when they have them.

Unit 10

Exercise 1

1 Angelo's father had a small business making wood products, particularly barrels for transporting liquids. **2** He had a team of four or five working for him. He was one of only two people in the town who carried a revolver to defend himself should he be attacked. And he managed to bring up a very large family. **3** The main difficulty was the very poor communications. To reach the railway he had to walk some 10–12 kilometres. In addition the journey was dangerous, since there were bandits in the area. He needed to be armed. **4** He feels that had his father been running a business in the North, where the conditions, and communications in particular, were so much better, he would have been considerably more successful. **5** Because Angelo's father not only had ten children of his own (Angelo was the youngest), he also brought up his brother's six children, after his brother's early death.

Exercise 2

era; c'era; faceva; si incontrava; ci telefonavamo; sapevamo; si raggruppava; passavamo; era.

Exercise 3

1 Enrico non *è andato* in spiaggia perché *aveva* la febbre. **2** Franco e Giovanna *hanno deciso* di sposarsi perché *erano* innamorati. **3** Marco *ha comprato* un regalo per Anna perché *era* il suo compleanno. **4** Filippo non *è andato* all'Università perché non *amava* studiare. **5** Francesca *ha telefonato* a Enzo perché *voleva* salutarlo.

Exercise 4

1 It took three days. It must be said it would probably take the best part of two by car even today. **2** There was no motorway in those days. In fact the motorway south of Naples to Reggio Calabria, the toe of Italy, was completed in the early 1970s. **3** The mountains with the hairpin bends as the road went up each mountain and then more bends down into the valleys between. They seemed never-ending, without a single viaduct.

Exercise 5

1 She was struck by the way the family was self-sufficient. **2** Olive press: *frantoio*; flour mill: *mulino per macinare* – to grind (the wheat).

Exercise 6

1 avevo vissuto; **2** Avevo cominciato; **3** avevamo deciso; **4** aveva letto; **5** si erano conosciuti.

Unit 11

Exercise 1

1 Because it is only relatively recently that it has become the national language and as yet not everyone has adequate mastery of it. **2** Because the national language gives them the means to broaden their knowledge. Books and newspapers are written in Italian. He could have added that radio and TV use Italian too. **3** Dialect is good for everyday communication and possibly enables some people to express themselves in a more lively way; but dialects are understood only in a limited geographical area and allow people to talk only about everyday things. They do not allow the expression of technical or philosophical concepts. **4** It would pose problems of choice of the variety to be taught. There are for instance difference versions of Sardinian dialect in various parts of Sardinia. There is no norm. And dialects have changed with people mixing in Italian with them so that they are no longer 'pure'. As for the minority languages such as Albanian and Catalan, which do you teach: that spoken in Italy or that spoken in Albania or Spain? **5** He suggests students be encouraged to research aspects of the local culture such as architecture, customs, beliefs, fables and legends, songs, proverbs, words which have fallen out of use, etc. **6** He thinks it important that people should be in touch with their cultural roots. Without roots, he says, people feel lost in an anonymous universal culture, which he implies has no real meaning.

Exercise 2

1 Il bagaglio a mano <u>va messo</u>. **2** Il telefonino <u>va spento</u>. **3** Lo schienale <u>va portato</u>. **4** Il tavolino <u>va chiuso</u>.

Exercise 3

1 <u>La frutta, la compro</u> al mercato. <u>La verdura, la compro</u> nel negozio sotto casa. **2** <u>I quotidiani, li leggo</u> durante la settimana. <u>I settimanali, li leggo</u> nel weekend. **3** <u>Le foto, le guardo</u> adesso. <u>Le diapositive, le guardo</u> con calma, dopo cena.

Exercise 4

(a) **1**d – riscrivere; **2**c – ripulire; **3**a – riscoprire, **4**b – ribattere

(b) **1** to forget; **2** misinformation (incorrect information intentionally given out, often on an international scale, deliberately to mislead); **3** inattention, absent-mindedness; **4** to hope; **5** able, in the sense of having the qualities needed for a specific role, also: particularly talented, suitable for a job; **6** to cancel (an appointment usually), also: deny (something one has said); **7** inopportune, untimely, inconvenient.

(c) **1** garbato. **2** cortese. **3** of a person who makes lots of grammatical mistakes, or of a piece of writing containing many grammatical mistakes, ungrammatical. **4** to remove the fat from something – a liquid, meat – when preparing food. **5** to take out of the oven, to serve up (can be to remove from the tin, of a cake for instance), also figuratively, to turn out lots of something, for instance books, films: sforna regolarmente un paio di libri ogni anno.

(d) **1** strapieno. **2** strapagato. **3** stracuocere. **4** strafare.

Exercise 5

1 True. Teresa relates this to show how very Neapolitan her family is. **2** True. She considers herself bilingual and is proud of speaking Neapolitan dialect really well. **3** False, she avoided it. She and Sandra agree that when they were young, using dialect was looked down on. **4** True. Nowadays, that is less true. Many people use dialect or Italian depending on the context. Using dialect can be a way of expressing belonging to the same community as others and many people enjoy the expressions and vocabulary dialect affords.

Exercise 6

1 She sees Paduan as a country dialect, used by people of limited education, working class. Venetian she sees as patrician, noble, literary. **2** She thinks it was a choice made because they saw themselves as educated, upper class.

Exercise 7

1 That they should definitely not teach Tuscan as the standard Italian since different varieties of Italian are now acceptable. There is no one standard variety. **2** That they can manipulate verbs correctly, even in the subjunctive. In other words, the grammar of the dialect is that of standard Italian.

Exercise 8

Marta *sperava* che Gianni
1 non *amasse* il calcio, e invece lui va a vedere la partita ogni domenica.
2 non *fosse* vegetariano, e invece lui detesta la carne. **3** *fosse* appassionato di musica latino-americana e *sapesse* suonare la chitarra, invece lui ama la musica classica e suona il pianoforte.

Gianni *sperava* che Maria
4 *fosse* bruna, e invece Maria ha i capelli rossi. **5** *avesse* la voce dolce, e invece ha una voce squillante e stentorea. **6** *amasse* viaggiare, e invece Maria ama passare le vacanze nella casa di campagna. **7** *adorasse* i ristoranti di pesce, invece Maria non sopporta l'odore del pesce.

Unit 12

Exercise 1

1 *Sarà*, at the end of the first paragraph. The future expresses a conjecture: 'Maybe, be that as it may'. **2** He considered it watery and insipid; and obviously disliked drinking from a styroform cup. Readers will know *espresso* is very concentrated and is served in a small china cup. **3** No smoking is allowed in a Starbucks bar. The names of some of the drinks served are unknown in Italy – e.g. mockacino; for others, the Americans, not unnaturally, pronounce the names in a way Italians find funny; they also order such things as a double espresso – Italians generally don't do this. They may have a number of coffees in a day, but the espresso is concentrated and the quantity is small. And Americans queue in an orderly manner, waiting their turn, not something Italians do willingly! They expect to pop in and out of a bar quickly. He also implies the inexperienced American barmen find the business of producing the coffees difficult. **4** Because the bar is an Italian phenomenon.

Exercise 2

1 conobbi. **2** Ebbe. **3** decidemmo. **4** lavorai. **5** chiamarono. **6** decisi. **7** rimase. **8** fece.

Exercise 3

1 One is seen from within Italy, the other from abroad. She develops this idea further in the second paragraph. **2** They are comedies, light but stylish. And they are having considerable success with the public in Italy. **3** Sergio Castellitto is a good actor, and doesn't overplay. Stefania Rocca acts intelligently and without exploiting her physical charms. **4** The themes are often about family or marital issues; but some also treat socio-political problems, depicting the real Italy. **5** She feels outside Italy audiences – and juries such as that of the Oscars – tend to go for films which, while being aesthetically very pleasing, depict a stereotypical Italy which does not reflect today's reality. **6** Intellectual, inward-looking, very much generational, left-wing. **7** That no one, outside Italy, perhaps, is interested in the real, deep, controversial Italy of today. By deep she seems to mean as opposed to the superficial Italy of films like *Il Postino*.

Exercise 4

1 La giovane donna che indossa un vestito nero è l'attrice Maria Grazia Cucinotta (personaggio B). **2** L'uomo che si ripara gli occhi dal sole è il regista Marco Tullio Giordana (personaggio D). **3** L'uomo che sorride, con la barba e abbronzato, è l'attore Diego Abatantuono (personaggio C). **4** La giovane donna che incrocia le braccia sul petto è l'attrice Stefania Rocca (personaggio F). **5** L'uomo che è seduto e sta applaudendo è l'attore e regista Nanni Moretti (personaggio E).

Exercise 5

1 The actress they gave the part of the heroine to in *Casomai* is called Stefania Rocca. **2** Roberto Benigni is an Italian actor who they gave an Oscar to a few years ago. **3** *Nuovo Cinema Paradiso* is an example of a film in which there are many Italian stereotypes. **4** *I cento passi* is a film with which Marco Tullio Giordana wanted to expose the Mafia.

Exercise 6

1b; **2**a.

Grammar index

conditional	84, 95–97, 183–185
form	95–96, 183–185
irregular	96, 184–185
regular	95–96, 183–184
modal verbs	94
use	97
future indicative	111–112, 183–185
form	111, 183–185
irregular	111, 184–185
regular	111, 183–184
use	112
gerund	73–75, 109–110
form	74
uses	74
with a pronoun	75
with **stare**	109–110
imperative	98–101, 185–186
abbreviated	100, 186
irregular	98, 100, 186
Lei form	98, 185
with pronouns	98
negative imperative	101, 185
plural	99, 185
tu form	100, 185
with pronouns	100
imperfect indicative	121–124, 186–187
form	122–123, 186–187
irregular	122–123, 187
regular	122, 186
use	123–124
imperfect subjunctive	143–144, 180–181
form	143, 180
irregular	143, 180
regular	143, 180
use	144, 181

modal verbs 81–82, 84–86
  form 82, 84, 85–86
    present indicative 82
    conditional 84
    perfect tense 85–86
  use 84–85
  with a pronoun 82
numbers 11–12
passive 134–135
  with **andare** 135
  with **essere** 134
  with **venire** 134
past definite 149–150, 187–188
  form 149–150, 187–188
    irregular 150, 188
    regular 149–150, 187
  use 150
past participle 55, 59, 66–67, 182–183
  irregular 59, 66–67, 182–183
  regular 55
perfect tense 55–57, 59–62, 181–183
  form 55
  use 55
  use with **per** + expression of time .. 62
  with **avere** or **essere** 56, 60, 181–182
  with transitive and intransitive verbs .. 56–57, 60
pluperfect indicative 128
  form 128
  use 128
possessive adjectives 28–29
  use with and without definite article .. 29
prefixes 137
  dis- 137
  im-/in- 137
  ri- 137
  s- 137
  stra- 137
present continuous tense 109–110
present indicative 3–7, 37–38, 174–175, 176–178
  form 3–5, 37–38, 174–175, 176–178

irregular	37–38, 176–178
regular	3–5, 174–175
use	5–7, 10–11
use with **da** + expresion of time	6–7
present subjunctive	41–45, 178–181
form	42–43, 178–180
irregular	43, 179–180
regular	42–43, 178
in relative clauses	102–103
use	41–42, 44–45, 181
pronouns	22–23, 29–30, 35–37, 40–41, 75, 82, 98, 100, 114–115, 154–155
agreement with past participle	60–61
ci and **vi**	29–30
combined	41
direct and indirect object pronouns	35–37, 190
ne	40–41
position with gerund	75
position with infinitive	75
position with informal imperative	100
position with modal verbs	82
position with past participle	75
position with polite imperative	98
reflexive pronouns	22–23, 114, 115, 176
relative pronouns	154–155
si passivante	115
si used as subject pronoun	114–115
subject pronouns	16–17, 190
question words	50, 190–191
reflexive verbs	22–23, 176
suffixes	31–32, 92–93
-**accio**/-**accia**	32
-**astro**/-**astra**	32
-**eggiante**	32
-**ello**/-**ella**	32
-**enza**	93
-**etto**/-**etta**	32
-**iccio**/-**iccia**	32
-**ino**	32
-**issimo**	32

-ita	93
-mento	93
-one/-ona	32
-tore/-trice	92
-uccio/-uccia	32
-zione	92
verbs followed by	70
a + infinitive	70, 189
di + infinitive	70, 189–190
simple infinitive	70, 189
subjunctive	41–42, 45, 144, 181